The One Minute
Pause Journal

The One Minute
Pause Journal

JOHN ELDREDGE

NELSON
BOOKS

An Imprint of Thomas Nelson

Library of Congress Cataloging-in-Publication Data

Names: Eldredge, John, 1960- author.
Title: The one minute pause journal / John Eldredge.
Description: Nashville, Tennessee : Nelson Books, [2022] | Summary: "New York Times bestselling author John Eldredge guides readers through a simple daily practice that will help them find the connection to God and small moments of peace during busy days that they crave"-- Provided by publisher.
Identifiers: LCCN 2021041776 | ISBN 9781400234356 (hardcover)
Subjects: LCSH: Spiritual life--Christianity--Meditations. | Spiritual journals--Authorship.
Classification: LCC BV4501.3 .E4258 2022 | DDC 248.4--dc23
LC record available at https://lccn.loc.gov/2021041776

Printed in the United States of America

22 23 24 25 26 LSC 10 9 8 7 6 5 4 3 2 1

Contents

The One Minute Pause Journal

S ometimes it's the simple things in life that mean the most. A birthday card can really cheer you up. When you are desperately thirsty, a glass of water can be the most refreshing thing in the world. A few moments of a favorite song can lift your heart, and a simple kiss can make your day.

And a pause can save your life.

This journal is based on two simple ideas, premises, or assumptions. The first is that the world has gone absolutely mad, and it's trying to take our souls with it. The second idea—and here's the similarity to a birthday card, to the kiss—is that through learning the grace of a recentering pause, we can find peace, develop perspective, and even thrive in the midst of the madness.

No one likes the current pace of life; we all feel as though we don't have enough time to get everything done, so we run faster and faster. The daily barrage of news and social media is overwhelming, but we're addicted to it and can't get off our phones. We've lost the ability to pace our lives in accordance with our souls—to stop, breathe, and give our beleaguered hearts a break. Honestly, we're asking our souls to live at the speed of our smartphones.

But you can pause for a minute; you can do it a couple times a day. It's a small, defiant act, and it will make a wonderful difference.

How It Began

In February 2020, one month before the COVID-19 pandemic and subsequent quarantines swept the earth, I released a simple little app that I felt would be helpful to folks who wanted to take better care of their souls. The app—called the One Minute Pause—became a lifeline for many people during a time of unusual pressure and stress. Since its release, more than 200,000 people have found the One Minute Pause practice to be an absolute game changer. Such a simple practice for such a big reward!

But for me, it began earlier.

I began to notice that when I pulled into the driveway at the end of my day, more often than not I was fried. I was spun up, wrung out, and in no condition to walk in my front door and love the people waiting there. So I began the practice of turning off my engine and laying my head on the steering wheel. I would simply breathe and pray, "Jesus—I give everyone and everything to you. I give everyone and everything to you, Lord." Instead of just blasting on with my day, I would sit there and pause, letting my soul settle down, or unburden, or catch up to me after the wild pace of the day. Taking that small pause was wonderful, and from that simple start a practice developed that eventually became an app and a core piece of my book *Get Your Life Back: Everyday Practices for a World Gone Mad*.

The Practice

This journal is devoted to the art of the Pause itself.

The practice is quite simple, with three basic steps. The first is release—letting things go, what I call Benevolent Detachment. The Pause begins with simply giving everything over to God, untangling our souls from the worries, projects, and even people that attach themselves to us like Velcro. (I'll explain more on each step in a moment.)

The next step is Union—we pray that our union with God would be restored. The human soul is nourished and healed through union with God. Not just faith in God, but the actual union of our being with his. Like a branch to a vine, as Jesus put it. We need a source of strength, wisdom, and life much greater than our own resources. That would be God's role. Ours is to come into consistent union with him.

Last is Restoration—we pray to be filled with the life and love of God. To be strengthened, refreshed, saturated.

Many people have asked for a physical expression of the One Minute Pause app experience. There's something powerful in being able to write things down, put words to stuff, to prepare our hearts for prayer. We've found there's magic to doing it twice a day, so the journal is broken into two parts for each day. Sometime during your morning and sometime during your afternoon or evening, take a moment to practice this simple, rejuvenating pause. Choose the time that is best for you. Some people will want to leave their journal at work, because it's during the middle of their workday that they find themselves the most spun up. It's quite common to practice the Pause around 10 a.m. and 2 p.m. But other friends of ours love to keep this journal at home, possibly on their nightstand, because they want to begin and end their day with the wonderful practices of detachment, union, and restoration. The choice is yours!

The Power Behind
a Simple Pause

L et's explore a bit more of the three steps to the Pause, to help you get the essence of Benevolent Detachment, Union, and Restoration. This way, when you enter the Pause, you'll have a richer idea of the experience we are after—an experience, I want to add, that unfolds over time as we get practiced at it. Allow me to borrow a few excerpts for your benefit from my book *Get Your Life Back*.

Benevolent Detachment

I've always been intrigued by Jesus' ability to just up and walk away from his world. Right there in the opening chapter of the Gospel of Mark, with excitement building and crowds swelling all round him, Jesus disappears. He just . . . leaves.

> Very early in the morning, while it was still dark, Jesus got up, left the
> house and went off to a solitary place, where he prayed. Simon and
> his companions went to look for him, and when they found him, they

exclaimed: "Everyone is looking for you!" Jesus replied, "Let us go somewhere else. . . ." (Mark 1:35–38)

Jesus models a freedom of heart I think every one of us would love to have. His ability to disengage himself from his world is so alluring. But we broken and burdened human beings get so caught up in the drama.

You're running late; you text a coworker or your boss a gentle explanation that your child woke up sick, and you had to arrange for care before you left for work. All you receive back is a one-word reply: *Okay.* What does it mean? Are they mad at you? They're probably mad at you; one word feels like they are. They didn't say, *Oh gosh, I'm so sorry; hope they are feeling better. Totally understand. No worries.* But they may also be driving and not supposed to text, and one word was all they could manage to let you know it's okay. But you know how all those possibilities can play out in your mind; so you worry over subtext and intended meaning.

In order to make room for God to fill the vessel of our soul, we have to begin moving out some of the unnecessary clutter that continually accumulates there—like the junk drawer in your kitchen. Everybody has a junk drawer, that black hole for car keys, pens, paper clips, gum, all the small flotsam and jetsam that accumulates over time. Our souls accumulate stuff, too, and pull it in like a magnet. And so, Augustine said, we must empty ourselves of all that fills us, so that we may be filled with what we are empty of. Over time I've found no better practice to help clear out my cluttered soul than the practice of Benevolent Detachment. The ability to let it go, walk away—not so much physically, but emotionally, soulfully.

Allow me to explain. We are aiming for release, turning whatever is burdening us into the hands of God and leaving it there. It's so easy to get caught up in the drama in unhealthy ways, and then we are unable to see clearly, set boundaries, respond freely. Every day, a few times a day, it is so healthy to stop and give it all over to God. Something as simple as:

- "Jesus—I give my mom to you, and her diagnosis."
- "I give that meeting to you, and all my frustration."
- "I give tonight's dinner with our neighbors to you."
- "I'm tired, Lord. I can't carry this, and I'm not supposed to. I release it all to you."

Are you tired? Worn out? Burned out on religion? Come to me. Get away with me and you'll recover your life. I'll show you how to take a real rest. Walk with me and work with me—watch how I do it. Learn the unforced rhythms of grace. I won't lay anything heavy or ill-fitting on you. Keep company with me and you'll learn to live freely and lightly. (Matthew 11:28–30 THE MESSAGE)

Now, pay attention here—Jesus said there is a way "to live freely and lightly."

His dear friend Peter echoed the invitation later in the New Testament:

Cast all your anxiety on him because he cares for you. (1 Peter 5:7)
Live carefree before God; he is most careful with you. (1 Peter 5:7
THE MESSAGE)

Carefree? The offer is a carefree life?! I love feeling carefree. Carefree is how I feel in the middle of vacation. People are desperately seeking the feeling of being carefree. I think all our dissociative patterns are signs of it—the video games, the virtual reality craze, the chemicals we use to feel unburdened. You can see human beings trying to disentangle in the popularity of the helpful book *Boundaries*, which has sold millions of copies. We're looking for a way to take back some healthy detachment in our lives.

You've got to release the world; you've got to release people, crises, trauma, intrigue, all of it. There has to be sometime in your day where you just let it all go. All the tragedy of the world, the heartbreak, the

Are you tired? Worn out?
Burned out on religion? Come
to me. Get away with me and
you'll recover your life. I'll show
you how to take a real rest.
Walk with me and work with
me—watch how I do it. Learn
the unforced rhythms of grace.
I won't lay anything heavy or
ill-fitting on you. Keep company
with me and you'll learn to live
freely and lightly.

—Matthew 11:28–30 THE MESSAGE

latest shooting, the most recent natural disaster—the soul was never meant to endure this. The soul was never meant to inhabit a world like this. It's way too much. Your soul is finite. You cannot carry the sorrows of the world. Only God can do that. Only he is infinite. Somewhere, sometime in your day, you've just got to release it. You've got to let it go.

Benevolent Detachment is going to take some practice. The One Minute Pause is a good place to start. "I give everyone and everything to you, God. I give everyone and everything to you." Often, I find I need to follow that up with some specifics: "I give my children to you," for I worry about them. "I give that meeting to you." "I give this book to you." As you do this, pay attention—your soul will tell you whether or not you're releasing. If the moment after you pray you find yourself mulling over the very thing you just released, you haven't released it. Go back and repeat the process until it feels that you have.

Now the beauty of the One Minute Pause is that you're asking your soul to only do this in the right now. This isn't about attaining some new level of sainthood. We're simply pausing, releasing, and as we get the hang of it, we really do get better at letting go and leaving it "let go."

Union with God

Jesus used the imagery of a vine and its branches to describe the nature of connection he offers us. The branch is united with the vine, and that allows the vine to provide life in all its forms to the branch: sustenance, strength, immunity, resilience. The result for the branch is blossoming fruitfulness, abundant life. I'm afraid our familiarity with the passage, or at least the phrase "I am the Vine," has dimmed the miraculous offer: if you want, your life can become one shared existence with the Son of God, through whom all things were created, who sustains this glorious world.

Being the brilliant teacher he is, Jesus then followed up this meta-phor with a second, one that ups the ante and drives home his sincerity with what was meant to be a startling comparison:

> I pray also for those who will believe in me through their message, that all of them may be one, Father, *just as you are in me and I am in you.* May they also be in us so that the world may believe that you have sent me. I have given them the glory that you gave me, *that they may be one as we are one*—I in them and you in me. (John 17:20–23, emphasis added)

To be clear, Jesus prayed that we would experience the same kind of united life and being with him, that he experienced with his Father. He reinforced how serious he is about this by asking his disciples to record this prayer for you, so that the startling force of it would be with us always, in black and white.

Over time, this extraordinary offer grew veiled through the lan-guage we adopted to explain Christian faith. Language tends to define, and sometimes limit, expectations. Currently, the common way to describe the essence of Christian experience in most circles would be along the lines of "have faith in Christ." A good thing to have, faith is, but the phrase carries connotations. You can have faith without having much personal experience; you can hold to a certain religious faith and not actually know God yourself (I've met many of these dear souls). I have faith in my surgeon, but I don't know him at all; we certainly don't share our life together. I'm grateful for his help, but we aren't anything like best friends. Evangelical teachers try to rectify the problem when they say things like, "Christianity is not a religion, it's a relationship." Which is closer to the truth.

But *union*, oneness, integrated being—that is something else altogether.

Your very being is made to be saturated with the being of God. You can have faith in God from a distance; you can have a "relation-ship" with Christ, but not be intimate. You can even find an intimacy

I pray also for those who will believe in me through their message, that all of them may be one, Father, just as you are in me and I am in you. *May they also be in us so that the world may believe that you have sent me. I have given them the glory* that you gave me, that they may be one as we are one—*I in them and you in me.*

—John 17:20–23, emphasis added

with Christ, or your Father, or the Holy Spirit, and not be inhabited, interwoven, saturated.

Press your palms and fingers flat together like someone praying. Your left palm represents God; your right palm you. This expression, I would say, is an expression of genuine intimacy. You and God are close. Now, while your palms remain pressed together, fold your fingers downward, so that the fingers of both hands become intertwined. This is an expression of deeper union, where your being and God's become intertwined. This entwining, interlacing, is what the hidden roots of the forest do. It might surprise some readers to hear me say this, but we are after much more than faith, even more than intimacy. We are after union, oneness—where our being and God's Being become intertwined. The substance of our life—our personality, our heart, our physicality, all our experience—is filled over time to saturation with the substance of God's life.

Now the world we live in constantly erodes our union with God. The frantic pace, the tsunami of information, the amount of time on our screens, the madness of it all. We must intentionally seek the restoration of our union with God, so I've found it very important to ask God to heal my union with him on a fairly regular basis. I use the One Minute Pause as the daily way back to God.

Restoration

At the end of any given day, most people come home in a state of exhaustion. Numb on our good days, fried more often than we admit. As Bilbo Baggins said in *The Fellowship of the Ring*, "I feel all thin, sort of stretched, like butter that has been scraped over too much bread."

> How priceless is your unfailing love, O God!
> People take refuge in the shadow of your wings.
> They feast on the abundance of your house;

How priceless is your unfailing love, O God!

People take refuge in the shadow of your wings.

They feast on the abundance of your house;

you give them drink from your river of delights.

For with you is the fountain of life.

—Psalm 36:7–9

you give them drink from your river of delights.
For with you is the fountain of life. (Psalm 36:7–9)

Now, if we had more of God, that would really help. We could draw upon his love and strength, his wisdom and resilience. After all, God is the fountain of life (Psalm 36:9). If we had more of his lavish life bubbling up in us, it would be a rescue in this soul-scorching hour.

But this frantic, volatile world constantly wilts the soul, dries it out like a raisin, making it almost impossible to receive the life God is pouring forth.

That's called a double bind.

I tried to find more of God, knowing if I only had a greater measure of his life in me, I'd be able to navigate this rough terrain. I was practicing the usual stuff—prayer, worship, scripture, sacrament. But still I felt . . . I don't know . . . shallow somehow. Sipping God with teaspoons, not drinking great gulps—wading, not swimming. My soul felt like a shallow rain puddle. But I know the soul isn't a shallow puddle at all; it's deep and vast, capable of symphonies and heroic courage. I wanted to be living from those deep places, but I felt trapped in the shoals.

It's no coincidence that one of the most important books on our world, and what technology is doing to us, is called *The Shallows: What the Internet Is Doing to Our Brains*. We're losing our ability to focus and pay attention longer than a few moments. We live at the depth of the text, the swipe, the "like." This isn't just an intellectual problem, it's a spiritual crisis. It's pretty hard to hear "deep calling unto deep" when we're forced into the shallows of our own hearts and souls by this frenetic world.

Jesus heard even my surface prayers; he came to my rescue and began to lead me into a number of helps and practices—what I would call graces. Simple things, like a One Minute Pause, that were accessible and surprising in their power to restore. Learning Benevolent Detachment, the ability to let things go. Allowing for some transition in my day, instead of just blasting from one thing to the next. Drinking in the beauty God was providing in quiet moments. My soul began to recover, feel better, do better—however you want to describe it. I began to enjoy my life with God so much more; I was finally experiencing the "more" of him I'd been wanting so much. I began to get my life back.

Then I connected the dots . . .

God wants to come to us and restore our lives. He really does. But if our souls are not well, it's almost impossible to receive him. Dry, scorched ground can't absorb the very rain it needs.

As C. S. Lewis explained in *The Problem of Pain*, "the soul is but a hollow which God fills." In place of *hollow* I like the word *vessel*, something beautiful and artistic. Our souls are exquisite vessels created by God for him to saturate. I picture the round, curved basin at the top of an elegant fountain, overflowing with water spilling down all sides, running over with unceasing life. Wasn't that the promise? "As Scripture has said, rivers of living water will flow from within them" (John 7:38).

And so it follows that if we can receive help for restoring and renewing our weary, besieged souls, we'll enjoy the fruits of happy souls (which are many and wonderful) and also be able to receive more of God (which is even more wonderful). We'll find the vibrancy and resiliency we crave as human beings, living waters welling up from deep within. And then— we'll get our lives back!

But the process needs to be accessible and sustainable. We've all tried exercise, diets, Bible study programs that began with vim and verve, but over time got shoved to the side, lost in the chaos. I have a gym membership; I rarely use it. There are those books I haven't finished, loads of podcasts too. Rest assured, the graces I am offering here are within reach of a normal life. I think you'll find them simple, sustainable, and refreshing.

God *wants* to strengthen and renew your soul; Jesus longs to give you more of himself. Come, you weary and heavy laden. "Are you tired? Worn out? Burned out on religion? Come to me. Get away with me and you'll recover your life . . . learn to live freely and lightly" (Matthew 11:28–30 THE MESSAGE). You can get your life back; you can live freely and lightly. The world may be harsh, but God is gentle; he knows what your life is like. What we need to do is put ourselves in places that allow us to receive his help.

So we finish our pause by asking Jesus to fill us:

Jesus, restore my Union with you. I receive your Love. I receive your Life. Strengthen me.

That's the basic model, but of course, by all means, use your own words too. Linger in prayer! Love God! This is a kick-starter that will get you going!

How to Use This Journal

L et me say loud and clear, before you even turn the page: *This should never feel like more pressure!*

This is meant to *relieve* you of the many pressures in your life, not add to them! So let's just agree from the start that we're not going to try and do this perfectly. There is no "perfectly." This is a practice, not a performance.

Now yes, there's a good bit of research that shows the regular practice of our habits produces the real benefits. I think after a week of using this journal you are going to notice a difference, feel refreshment coming into your soul. After a month, most people report that they are looking forward to, even craving, their next Pause. And after several months—you'll love this so much it will become an indispensable part of your routine. A very life-giving part of your routine!

Oh, and though we call this the One Minute Pause, that's not a rule either. Some days one minute is all I have; other days I find I need several minutes to practice the Pause. There is no law here; listen to your soul. (Incidentally, when we built the app, we created a one-minute, three-minute, and five-minute version of the Pause. The three-minute version was our personal favorite, if that helps you set expectations for yourself. Three minutes goes by pretty quick! However, my team strongly encouraged me to include a ten-minute version too. I thought to myself,

No way; nobody has ten minutes for this. But as it turns out, the ten-minute version is the second-most-used Pause on the app!)

Having a physical expression of the Pause here in your hands allows you to do two things—"Name" the things you need and the things you need to let go of, and then ask for those things. Your "a.m." and "p.m." pauses begin with detachment, release—naming the things that on this particular day you feel you really need to get off your back or your mind, your heart.

As I enter a new day, what do I need to let go of—what is weighing on my heart?

The Thompson presentation

Danny and school

Getting my car in

Having named them in writing, you pause and give them over to God. Again—never perfectly, never thoroughly, but each time we practice this, we really do grow in our ability to release things and not carry them all on our shoulders.

The second step of the Pause is to ask Jesus for the things you need in this particular moment, on this particular day. The helpfulness of this step is partly in tuning into our own needs because, truth be told, we don't always know what it is we need. So as you pause, just let your heart speak—if I could ask Jesus for anything right now, what would I ask for?

What do I need from God today?

Help in letting go!

Wisdom for the presentation

Peace!

Hope!

Something to look forward to

And then we finish by asking for more of God—our deepest need and greatest joy!

Okay, here we go.

Again, these practices come from a book I wrote on soul care called *Get Your Life Back*. If you enjoy this journal, you might want to pick that book up. It has a number of other life-giving practices in it that you'll love!

Be still, and know that I am God.

—PSALM 46:10

AM

Begin with settling down. Take a long breath.

As I enter a new day, what do I need to let go of—what is weighing on my heart?

_____

_____

_____

_____

Pause, and give it to God. Let it go.

What do I need from God today?

_____

_____

_____

_____

Pause, and ask for it.

God promises to fill and strengthen you. Receive it.

Jesus, restore my Union with you. I receive your Love. I receive your Life. Strengthen me.

Linger there for a moment.

Where are your thoughts running right now?

PM

Begin with settling down. Take a long breath.

To enter this afternoon or evening with peace, what do I need to let go of? (Do any worries, fears, or regrets come to mind?)

_____

_____

_____

_____

Pause, and give it to God. Let it go.

At this point in my afternoon or evening, what do I need from God?

_____

_____

_____

_____

Pause, and ask.

God promises to restore your soul. Let him.

Jesus, restore my Union with you. Restore my soul. Saturate me with your Love; saturate me with your Life.

Linger there for a moment.

Peace I leave with you, My peace I give to you.
—JOHN 14:27 NKJV

AM

Begin with settling down. Take a long breath.

As I enter a new day, what do I need to let go of—what is weighing on my heart?

_____

_____

_____

_____

Pause, and give it to God. Let it go.

What do I need from God today?

_____

_____

_____

_____

Pause, and ask for it.

God promises to fill and strengthen you. Receive it.

Jesus, restore my Union with you. I receive your Love. I receive your Life. Strengthen me.

Linger there for a moment.

The world is trying to steal your peace. Don't let it!

PM

Begin with settling down. Take a long breath.

To enter this afternoon or evening with peace, what do I need to let go of? (Do any worries, fears, or regrets come to mind?)

_____

_____

_____

_____

Pause, and give it to God. Let it go.

At this point in my afternoon or evening, what do I need from God?

_____

_____

_____

_____

Pause, and ask.

God promises to restore your soul. Let him.

Jesus, restore my Union with you. Restore my soul. Saturate me with your Love; saturate me with your Life.

Linger there for a moment.

I have given them the glory that you gave
me, that they may be one as we are one.
—John 17:22

AM

Begin with settling down. Take a long breath.

As I enter a new day, what do I need to let go of—what is weighing on
my heart?

_____

_____

_____

_____

Pause, and give it to God. Let it go.

What do I need from God today?

_____

_____

_____

_____

Pause, and ask for it.

God promises to fill and strengthen you. Receive it.

Jesus, restore my Union with you. I receive your Love. I receive your
Life. Strengthen me.

Linger there for a moment.

Your soul is designed for union with God!

PM

Begin with settling down. Take a long breath.

To enter this afternoon or evening with peace, what do I need to let go of? (Do any worries, fears, or regrets come to mind?)

_____

_____

_____

_____

Pause, and give it to God. Let it go.

At this point in my afternoon or evening, what do I need from God?

_____

_____

_____

_____

Pause, and ask.

God promises to restore your soul. Let him.

Jesus, restore my Union with you. Restore my soul. Saturate me with your Love; saturate me with your Life.

Linger there for a moment.

> That you may be filled to the measure
> of all the fullness of God.
> —EPHESIANS 3:19

AM

Begin with settling down. Take a long breath.

As I enter a new day, what do I need to let go of—what is weighing on my heart?

_____

_____

_____

_____

Pause, and give it to God. Let it go.

What do I need from God today?

_____

_____

_____

_____

Pause, and ask for it.

God promises to fill and strengthen you. Receive it.

Jesus, restore my Union with you. I receive your Love. I receive your Life. Strengthen me.

Linger there for a moment.

God really does want to fill you!

PM

Begin with settling down. Take a long breath.

To enter this afternoon or evening with peace, what do I need to let go of? (Do any worries, fears, or regrets come to mind?)

_____

_____

_____

_____

Pause, and give it to God. Let it go.

At this point in my afternoon or evening, what do I need from God?

_____

_____

_____

_____

Pause, and ask.

God promises to restore your soul. Let him.

Jesus, restore my Union with you. Restore my soul. Saturate me with your Love; saturate me with your Life.

Linger there for a moment.

Don't let the world around you squeeze
you into its own mould.
—ROMANS 12:2 PHILLIPS

AM

Begin with settling down. Take a long breath.

As I enter a new day, what do I need to let go of—what is weighing on
my heart?

_____

_____

_____

_____

Pause, and give it to God. Let it go.

What do I need from God today?

_____

_____

_____

_____

Pause, and ask for it.

God promises to fill and strengthen you. Receive it.

Jesus, restore my Union with you. I receive your Love. I receive your
Life. Strengthen me.

Linger there for a moment.

The world is toxic; pause and detox.

PM

Begin with settling down. Take a long breath.

To enter this afternoon or evening with peace, what do I need to let go of? (Do any worries, fears, or regrets come to mind?)

_____

_____

_____

_____

Pause, and give it to God. Let it go.

At this point in my afternoon or evening, what do I need from God?

_____

_____

_____

_____

Pause, and ask.

God promises to restore your soul. Let him.

Jesus, restore my Union with you. Restore my soul. Saturate me with your Love; saturate me with your Life.

Linger there for a moment.

He restores my soul.

—PSALM 23:3 NKJV

AM

Begin with settling down. Take a long breath.

As I enter a new day, what do I need to let go of—what is weighing on my heart?

_____

_____

_____

_____

Pause, and give it to God. Let it go.

What do I need from God today?

_____

_____

_____

_____

Pause, and ask for it.

God promises to fill and strengthen you. Receive it.

Jesus, restore my Union with you. I receive your Love. I receive your Life. Strengthen me.

Linger there for a moment.

Jesus knows you need restoring. Pause, and receive.

PM

Begin with settling down. Take a long breath.

To enter this afternoon or evening with peace, what do I need to let go of? (Do any worries, fears, or regrets come to mind?)

_____

_____

_____

_____

Pause, and give it to God. Let it go.

At this point in my afternoon or evening, what do I need from God?

_____

_____

_____

_____

Pause, and ask.

God promises to restore your soul. Let him.

Jesus, restore my Union with you. Restore my soul. Saturate me with your Love; saturate me with your Life.

Linger there for a moment.

Whoever believes in me, as Scripture has said,
rivers of living water will flow from within them.
—JOHN 7:38

AM

Begin with settling down. Take a long breath.

As I enter a new day, what do I need to let go of—what is weighing on
my heart?

_____

_____

_____

_____

Pause, and give it to God. Let it go.

What do I need from God today?

_____

_____

_____

_____

Pause, and ask for it.

God promises to fill and strengthen you. Receive it.

Jesus, restore my Union with you. I receive your Love. I receive your
Life. Strengthen me.

Linger there for a moment.

Let God fill you with rivers of his life.

PM

Begin with settling down. Take a long breath.

To enter this afternoon or evening with peace, what do I need to let go of? (Do any worries, fears, or regrets come to mind?)

_____

_____

_____

_____

Pause, and give it to God. Let it go.

At this point in my afternoon or evening, what do I need from God?

_____

_____

_____

_____

Pause, and ask.

God promises to restore your soul. Let him.

Jesus, restore my Union with you. Restore my soul. Saturate me with your Love; saturate me with your Life.

Linger there for a moment.

In this world you will have trouble. But take
heart! I have overcome the world.
—JOHN 16:33

AM

Begin with settling down. Take a long breath.

As I enter a new day, what do I need to let go of—what is weighing on
my heart?

_____

_____

_____

_____

Pause, and give it to God. Let it go.

What do I need from God today?

_____

_____

_____

_____

Pause, and ask for it.

God promises to fill and strengthen you. Receive it.

Jesus, restore my Union with you. I receive your Love. I receive your
Life. Strengthen me.

Linger there for a moment.

You have got to let the world go. Every day.

PM

Begin with settling down. Take a long breath.

To enter this afternoon or evening with peace, what do I need to let go of? (Do any worries, fears, or regrets come to mind?)

_____

_____

_____

_____

Pause, and give it to God. Let it go.

At this point in my afternoon or evening, what do I need from God?

_____

_____

_____

_____

Pause, and ask.

God promises to restore your soul. Let him.

Jesus, restore my Union with you. Restore my soul. Saturate me with your Love; saturate me with your Life.

Linger there for a moment.

For my yoke is easy and my burden is light.
—MATTHEW 11:30

AM

Begin with settling down. Take a long breath.

As I enter a new day, what do I need to let go of—what is weighing on my heart?

_____

_____

_____

_____

Pause, and give it to God. Let it go.

What do I need from God today?

_____

_____

_____

_____

Pause, and ask for it.

God promises to fill and strengthen you. Receive it.

Jesus, restore my Union with you. I receive your Love. I receive your Life. Strengthen me.

Linger there for a moment.

Don't take any yoke upon you but the yoke of Jesus.

PM

Begin with settling down. Take a long breath.

To enter this afternoon or evening with peace, what do I need to let go of? (Do any worries, fears, or regrets come to mind?)

_____

_____

_____

_____

Pause, and give it to God. Let it go.

At this point in my afternoon or evening, what do I need from God?

_____

_____

_____

_____

Pause, and ask.

God promises to restore your soul. Let him.

Jesus, restore my Union with you. Restore my soul. Saturate me with your Love; saturate me with your Life.

Linger there for a moment.

For apart from me you can do nothing.

—JOHN 15:5 NLT

AM

Begin with settling down. Take a long breath.

As I enter a new day, what do I need to let go of—what is weighing on my heart?

_____

_____

_____

_____

Pause, and give it to God. Let it go.

What do I need from God today?

_____

_____

_____

_____

Pause, and ask for it.

God promises to fill and strengthen you. Receive it.

Jesus, restore my Union with you. I receive your Love. I receive your Life. Strengthen me.

Linger there for a moment.

The secret of Christianity is the life of Christ in you.

PM

Begin with settling down. Take a long breath.

To enter this afternoon or evening with peace, what do I need to let go of? (Do any worries, fears, or regrets come to mind?)

_____

_____

_____

_____

Pause, and give it to God. Let it go.

At this point in my afternoon or evening, what do I need from God?

_____

_____

_____

_____

Pause, and ask.

God promises to restore your soul. Let him.

Jesus, restore my Union with you. Restore my soul. Saturate me with your Love; saturate me with your Life.

Linger there for a moment.

Give all your worries and cares to
God, for he cares about you.
—1 PETER 5:7 NLT

AM

Begin with settling down. Take a long breath.

As I enter a new day, what do I need to let go of—what is weighing on my heart?

_____

_____

_____

_____

Pause, and give it to God. Let it go.

What do I need from God today?

_____

_____

_____

_____

Pause, and ask for it.

God promises to fill and strengthen you. Receive it.

Jesus, restore my Union with you. I receive your Love. I receive your Life. Strengthen me.

Linger there for a moment.

Give everyone and everything over to God. Every day.

PM

Begin with settling down. Take a long breath.

To enter this afternoon or evening with peace, what do I need to let go of? (Do any worries, fears, or regrets come to mind?)

_____

_____

_____

_____

Pause, and give it to God. Let it go.

At this point in my afternoon or evening, what do I need from God?

_____

_____

_____

_____

Pause, and ask.

God promises to restore your soul. Let him.

Jesus, restore my Union with you. Restore my soul. Saturate me with your Love; saturate me with your Life.

Linger there for a moment.

Remain in me, and I will remain in you.

—JOHN 15:4 NLT

AM

Begin with settling down. Take a long breath.

As I enter a new day, what do I need to let go of—what is weighing on my heart?

_____

_____

_____

_____

Pause, and give it to God. Let it go.

What do I need from God today?

_____

_____

_____

_____

Pause, and ask for it.

God promises to fill and strengthen you. Receive it.

Jesus, restore my Union with you. I receive your Love. I receive your Life. Strengthen me.

Linger there for a moment.

Each pause we are choosing to come back to God.

PM

Begin with settling down. Take a long breath.

To enter this afternoon or evening with peace, what do I need to let go of? (Do any worries, fears, or regrets come to mind?)

_____

_____

_____

_____

Pause, and give it to God. Let it go.

At this point in my afternoon or evening, what do I need from God?

_____

_____

_____

_____

Pause, and ask.

God promises to restore your soul. Let him.

Jesus, restore my Union with you. Restore my soul. Saturate me with your Love; saturate me with your Life.

Linger there for a moment.

[He] satisfies your desires with good things so
that your youth is renewed like the eagle's.
—PSALM 103:5

AM

Begin with settling down. Take a long breath.

As I enter a new day, what do I need to let go of—what is weighing on my heart?

_____

_____

_____

_____

Pause, and give it to God. Let it go.

What do I need from God today?

_____

_____

_____

_____

Pause, and ask for it.

God promises to fill and strengthen you. Receive it.

Jesus, restore my Union with you. I receive your Love. I receive your Life. Strengthen me.

Linger there for a moment.

We all need renewing. Every day.

PM

Begin with settling down. Take a long breath.

To enter this afternoon or evening with peace, what do I need to let go of? (Do any worries, fears, or regrets come to mind?)

_____

_____

_____

_____

Pause, and give it to God. Let it go.

At this point in my afternoon or evening, what do I need from God?

_____

_____

_____

_____

Pause, and ask.

God promises to restore your soul. Let him.

Jesus, restore my Union with you. Restore my soul. Saturate me with your Love; saturate me with your Life.

Linger there for a moment.

You prepare a table before me . . . my cup overflows.
—PSALM 23:5

AM

Begin with settling down. Take a long breath.

As I enter a new day, what do I need to let go of—what is weighing on my heart?

_____

_____

_____

_____

Pause, and give it to God. Let it go.

What do I need from God today?

_____

_____

_____

_____

Pause, and ask for it.

God promises to fill and strengthen you. Receive it.

Jesus, restore my Union with you. I receive your Love. I receive your Life. Strengthen me.

Linger there for a moment.

God really does have abundance for
you. First, abundance of himself.

PM

Begin with settling down. Take a long breath.

To enter this afternoon or evening with peace, what do I need to let go
of? (Do any worries, fears, or regrets come to mind?)

_____

_____

_____

_____

Pause, and give it to God. Let it go.

At this point in my afternoon or evening, what do I need from God?

_____

_____

_____

_____

Pause, and ask.

God promises to restore your soul. Let him.

Jesus, restore my Union with you. Restore my soul. Saturate me with
your Love; saturate me with your Life.

Linger there for a moment.

No one can redeem the life of another or
give to God a ransom for them.
—PSALM 49:7

AM

Begin with settling down. Take a long breath.

As I enter a new day, what do I need to let go of—what is weighing on
my heart?

_____

_____

_____

_____

Pause, and give it to God. Let it go.

What do I need from God today?

_____

_____

_____

_____

Pause, and ask for it.

God promises to fill and strengthen you. Receive it.

Jesus, restore my Union with you. I receive your Love. I receive your
Life. Strengthen me.

Linger there for a moment.

You really can't save anyone; only God is Savior.

PM

Begin with settling down. Take a long breath.

To enter this afternoon or evening with peace, what do I need to let go of? (Do any worries, fears, or regrets come to mind?)

_____

_____

_____

_____

Pause, and give it to God. Let it go.

At this point in my afternoon or evening, what do I need from God?

_____

_____

_____

_____

Pause, and ask.

God promises to restore your soul. Let him.

Jesus, restore my Union with you. Restore my soul. Saturate me with your Love; saturate me with your Life.

Linger there for a moment.

If you remain in me and I in you,
you will bear much fruit.
—JOHN 15:5

AM

Begin with settling down. Take a long breath.

As I enter a new day, what do I need to let go of—what is weighing on my heart?

_____

_____

_____

_____

Pause, and give it to God. Let it go.

What do I need from God today?

_____

_____

_____

_____

Pause, and ask for it.

God promises to fill and strengthen you. Receive it.

Jesus, restore my Union with you. I receive your Love. I receive your Life. Strengthen me.

Linger there for a moment.

Jesus—I choose to stay in you today.

PM

Begin with settling down. Take a long breath.

To enter this afternoon or evening with peace, what do I need to let go of? (Do any worries, fears, or regrets come to mind?)

_____

_____

_____

_____

Pause, and give it to God. Let it go.

At this point in my afternoon or evening, what do I need from God?

_____

_____

_____

_____

Pause, and ask.

God promises to restore your soul. Let him.

Jesus, restore my Union with you. Restore my soul. Saturate me with your Love; saturate me with your Life.

Linger there for a moment.

He satisfies the thirsty and fills the
hungry with good things.
—PSALM 107:9

AM

Begin with settling down. Take a long breath.

As I enter a new day, what do I need to let go of—what is weighing on
my heart?

_____

_____

_____

_____

Pause, and give it to God. Let it go.

What do I need from God today?

_____

_____

_____

_____

Pause, and ask for it.

God promises to fill and strengthen you. Receive it.

Jesus, restore my Union with you. I receive your Love. I receive your
Life. Strengthen me.

Linger there for a moment.

Only God can satisfy our thirsty souls.

PM

Begin with settling down. Take a long breath.

To enter this afternoon or evening with peace, what do I need to let go of? (Do any worries, fears, or regrets come to mind?)

_____

_____

_____

_____

Pause, and give it to God. Let it go.

At this point in my afternoon or evening, what do I need from God?

_____

_____

_____

_____

Pause, and ask.

God promises to restore your soul. Let him.

Jesus, restore my Union with you. Restore my soul. Saturate me with your Love; saturate me with your Life.

Linger there for a moment.

For everyone born of God overcomes the world.
—1 JOHN 5:4

AM

Begin with settling down. Take a long breath.

As I enter a new day, what do I need to let go of—what is weighing on my heart?

_____

_____

_____

_____

Pause, and give it to God. Let it go.

What do I need from God today?

_____

_____

_____

_____

Pause, and ask for it.

God promises to fill and strengthen you. Receive it.

Jesus, restore my Union with you. I receive your Love. I receive your Life. Strengthen me.

Linger there for a moment.

Father—help me overcome the madness of the world.

PM

Begin with settling down. Take a long breath.

To enter this afternoon or evening with peace, what do I need to let go of? (Do any worries, fears, or regrets come to mind?)

_____

_____

_____

_____

Pause, and give it to God. Let it go.

At this point in my afternoon or evening, what do I need from God?

_____

_____

_____

_____

Pause, and ask.

God promises to restore your soul. Let him.

Jesus, restore my Union with you. Restore my soul. Saturate me with your Love; saturate me with your Life.

Linger there for a moment.

I and the Father are one.

—John 10:30

AM

Begin with settling down. Take a long breath.

As I enter a new day, what do I need to let go of—what is weighing on my heart?

_____

_____

_____

_____

Pause, and give it to God. Let it go.

What do I need from God today?

_____

_____

_____

_____

Pause, and ask for it.

God promises to fill and strengthen you. Receive it.

Jesus, restore my Union with you. I receive your Love. I receive your Life. Strengthen me.

Linger there for a moment.

Make me one with you, God.

PM

Begin with settling down. Take a long breath.

To enter this afternoon or evening with peace, what do I need to let go of? (Do any worries, fears, or regrets come to mind?)

_____

_____

_____

_____

Pause, and give it to God. Let it go.

At this point in my afternoon or evening, what do I need from God?

_____

_____

_____

_____

Pause, and ask.

God promises to restore your soul. Let him.

Jesus, restore my Union with you. Restore my soul. Saturate me with your Love; saturate me with your Life.

Linger there for a moment.

Made whole and holy by his love.

AM

Begin with settling down. Take a long breath.

As I enter a new day, what do I need to let go of—what is weighing on my heart?

_____

_____

_____

_____

Pause, and give it to God. Let it go.

What do I need from God today?

_____

_____

_____

_____

Pause, and ask for it.

God promises to fill and strengthen you. Receive it.

Jesus, restore my Union with you. I receive your Love. I receive your Life. Strengthen me.

Linger there for a moment.

God wants to make you whole and holy, by his love.

PM

Begin with settling down. Take a long breath.

To enter this afternoon or evening with peace, what do I need to let go of? (Do any worries, fears, or regrets come to mind?)

_____

_____

_____

_____

Pause, and give it to God. Let it go.

At this point in my afternoon or evening, what do I need from God?

_____

_____

_____

_____

Pause, and ask.

God promises to restore your soul. Let him.

Jesus, restore my Union with you. Restore my soul. Saturate me with your Love; saturate me with your Life.

Linger there for a moment.

"For I know the plans I have for you," says the
Lord. ". . . to give you a future and a hope."
—Jeremiah 29:11 nlt

AM

Begin with settling down. Take a long breath.

As I enter a new day, what do I need to let go of—what is weighing on
my heart?

_____

_____

_____

_____

Pause, and give it to God. Let it go.

What do I need from God today?

_____

_____

_____

_____

Pause, and ask for it.

God promises to fill and strengthen you. Receive it.

Jesus, restore my Union with you. I receive your Love. I receive your
Life. Strengthen me.

Linger there for a moment.

You can rest in the goodness of God today.

PM

Begin with settling down. Take a long breath.

To enter this afternoon or evening with peace, what do I need to let go of? (Do any worries, fears, or regrets come to mind?)

_____

_____

_____

_____

Pause, and give it to God. Let it go.

At this point in my afternoon or evening, what do I need from God?

_____

_____

_____

_____

Pause, and ask.

God promises to restore your soul. Let him.

Jesus, restore my Union with you. Restore my soul. Saturate me with your Love; saturate me with your Life.

Linger there for a moment.

Nothing can ever separate us from God's love.
—ROMANS 8:38 NLT

AM

Begin with settling down. Take a long breath.

As I enter a new day, what do I need to let go of—what is weighing on my heart?

_____

_____

_____

_____

Pause, and give it to God. Let it go.

What do I need from God today?

_____

_____

_____

_____

Pause, and ask for it.

God promises to fill and strengthen you. Receive it.

Jesus, restore my Union with you. I receive your Love. I receive your Life. Strengthen me.

Linger there for a moment.

The love of God is our greatest source of peace.

PM

Begin with settling down. Take a long breath.

To enter this afternoon or evening with peace, what do I need to let go of? (Do any worries, fears, or regrets come to mind?)

_____

_____

_____

_____

Pause, and give it to God. Let it go.

At this point in my afternoon or evening, what do I need from God?

_____

_____

_____

_____

Pause, and ask.

God promises to restore your soul. Let him.

Jesus, restore my Union with you. Restore my soul. Saturate me with your Love; saturate me with your Life.

Linger there for a moment.

It is for freedom that Christ has set us free.
—GALATIANS 5:1

AM

Begin with settling down. Take a long breath.

As I enter a new day, what do I need to let go of—what is weighing on my heart?

_____

_____

_____

_____

Pause, and give it to God. Let it go.

What do I need from God today?

_____

_____

_____

_____

Pause, and ask for it.

God promises to fill and strengthen you. Receive it.

Jesus, restore my Union with you. I receive your Love. I receive your Life. Strengthen me.

Linger there for a moment.

Remember—don't let any "yoke" come
upon you but the yoke of Jesus.

PM

Begin with settling down. Take a long breath.

To enter this afternoon or evening with peace, what do I need to let go
of? (Do any worries, fears, or regrets come to mind?)

_____

_____

_____

_____

Pause, and give it to God. Let it go.

At this point in my afternoon or evening, what do I need from God?

_____

_____

_____

_____

Pause, and ask.

God promises to restore your soul. Let him.

Jesus, restore my Union with you. Restore my soul. Saturate me with
your Love; saturate me with your Life.

Linger there for a moment.

God . . . gives us all we need for our enjoyment.

—1 TIMOTHY 6:17 NLT

AM

Begin with settling down. Take a long breath.

As I enter a new day, what do I need to let go of—what is weighing on my heart?

_____

_____

_____

_____

Pause, and give it to God. Let it go.

What do I need from God today?

_____

_____

_____

_____

Pause, and ask for it.

God promises to fill and strengthen you. Receive it.

Jesus, restore my Union with you. I receive your Love. I receive your Life. Strengthen me.

Linger there for a moment.

We need to hang on to this: God is generous.

PM

Begin with settling down. Take a long breath.

To enter this afternoon or evening with peace, what do I need to let go of? (Do any worries, fears, or regrets come to mind?)

_____

_____

_____

_____

Pause, and give it to God. Let it go.

At this point in my afternoon or evening, what do I need from God?

_____

_____

_____

_____

Pause, and ask.

God promises to restore your soul. Let him.

Jesus, restore my Union with you. Restore my soul. Saturate me with your Love; saturate me with your Life.

Linger there for a moment.

I have come that they may have
life, and have it to the full.
—JOHN 10:10

AM

Begin with settling down. Take a long breath.

As I enter a new day, what do I need to let go of—what is weighing on
my heart?

_____

_____

_____

_____

Pause, and give it to God. Let it go.

What do I need from God today?

_____

_____

_____

_____

Pause, and ask for it.

God promises to fill and strengthen you. Receive it.

Jesus, restore my Union with you. I receive your Love. I receive your
Life. Strengthen me.

Linger there for a moment.

Fullness comes as we unite ourselves with Jesus.

PM

Begin with settling down. Take a long breath.

To enter this afternoon or evening with peace, what do I need to let go of? (Do any worries, fears, or regrets come to mind?)

_____

_____

_____

_____

Pause, and give it to God. Let it go.

At this point in my afternoon or evening, what do I need from God?

_____

_____

_____

_____

Pause, and ask.

God promises to restore your soul. Let him.

Jesus, restore my Union with you. Restore my soul. Saturate me with your Love; saturate me with your Life.

Linger there for a moment.

As you received Christ Jesus as Lord,
continue to live your lives in him.
—COLOSSIANS 2:6

AM

Begin with settling down. Take a long breath.

As I enter a new day, what do I need to let go of—what is weighing on my heart?

_____

_____

_____

_____

Pause, and give it to God. Let it go.

What do I need from God today?

_____

_____

_____

_____

Pause, and ask for it.

God promises to fill and strengthen you. Receive it.

Jesus, restore my Union with you. I receive your Love. I receive your Life. Strengthen me.

Linger there for a moment.

You can't enjoy all God has for you
unless you remain in him.

PM

Begin with settling down. Take a long breath.

To enter this afternoon or evening with peace, what do I need to let go
of? (Do any worries, fears, or regrets come to mind?)

_____

_____

_____

_____

Pause, and give it to God. Let it go.

At this point in my afternoon or evening, what do I need from God?

_____

_____

_____

_____

Pause, and ask.

God promises to restore your soul. Let him.

Jesus, restore my Union with you. Restore my soul. Saturate me with
your Love; saturate me with your Life.

Linger there for a moment.

Stop doubting and believe.
—John 20:27

AM

Begin with settling down. Take a long breath.

As I enter a new day, what do I need to let go of—what is weighing on my heart?

_____

_____

_____

_____

Pause, and give it to God. Let it go.

What do I need from God today?

_____

_____

_____

_____

Pause, and ask for it.

God promises to fill and strengthen you. Receive it.

Jesus, restore my Union with you. I receive your Love. I receive your Life. Strengthen me.

Linger there for a moment.

Doubt is "in" because it feels authentic.
But Jesus wants you to believe.

PM

Begin with settling down. Take a long breath.

To enter this afternoon or evening with peace, what do I need to let go of? (Do any worries, fears, or regrets come to mind?)

_____

_____

_____

_____

Pause, and give it to God. Let it go.

At this point in my afternoon or evening, what do I need from God?

_____

_____

_____

_____

Pause, and ask.

God promises to restore your soul. Let him.

Jesus, restore my Union with you. Restore my soul. Saturate me with your Love; saturate me with your Life.

Linger there for a moment.

Fix your attention on God. You'll be
changed from the inside out.
—ROMANS 12:2 THE MESSAGE

AM

Begin with settling down. Take a long breath.

As I enter a new day, what do I need to let go of—what is weighing on
my heart?

_____

_____

_____

_____

Pause, and give it to God. Let it go.

What do I need from God today?

_____

_____

_____

_____

Pause, and ask for it.

God promises to fill and strengthen you. Receive it.

Jesus, restore my Union with you. I receive your Love. I receive your
Life. Strengthen me.

Linger there for a moment.

God's mission is to heal us as human beings.

PM

Begin with settling down. Take a long breath.

To enter this afternoon or evening with peace, what do I need to let go of? (Do any worries, fears, or regrets come to mind?)

_____

_____

_____

_____

Pause, and give it to God. Let it go.

At this point in my afternoon or evening, what do I need from God?

_____

_____

_____

_____

Pause, and ask.

God promises to restore your soul. Let him.

Jesus, restore my Union with you. Restore my soul. Saturate me with your Love; saturate me with your Life.

Linger there for a moment.

Do not let your hearts be troubled and do not be afraid.
—JOHN 14:27

AM

Begin with settling down. Take a long breath.

As I enter a new day, what do I need to let go of—what is weighing on my heart?

_____

_____

_____

_____

Pause, and give it to God. Let it go.

What do I need from God today?

_____

_____

_____

_____

Pause, and ask for it.

God promises to fill and strengthen you. Receive it.

Jesus, restore my Union with you. I receive your Love. I receive your Life. Strengthen me.

Linger there for a moment.

You have a say in what your heart gives way to.

PM

Begin with settling down. Take a long breath.

To enter this afternoon or evening with peace, what do I need to let go of? (Do any worries, fears, or regrets come to mind?)

_____

_____

_____

_____

Pause, and give it to God. Let it go.

At this point in my afternoon or evening, what do I need from God?

_____

_____

_____

_____

Pause, and ask.

God promises to restore your soul. Let him.

Jesus, restore my Union with you. Restore my soul. Saturate me with your Love; saturate me with your Life.

Linger there for a moment.

The unfailing love of the LORD fills the earth.
—PSALM 33:5 NLT

AM

Begin with settling down. Take a long breath.

As I enter a new day, what do I need to let go of—what is weighing on my heart?

_____

_____

_____

_____

Pause, and give it to God. Let it go.

What do I need from God today?

_____

_____

_____

_____

Pause, and ask for it.

God promises to fill and strengthen you. Receive it.

Jesus, restore my Union with you. I receive your Love. I receive your Life. Strengthen me.

Linger there for a moment.

God will be faithful to you today.

PM

Begin with settling down. Take a long breath.

To enter this afternoon or evening with peace, what do I need to let go of? (Do any worries, fears, or regrets come to mind?)

_____

_____

_____

_____

Pause, and give it to God. Let it go.

At this point in my afternoon or evening, what do I need from God?

_____

_____

_____

_____

Pause, and ask.

God promises to restore your soul. Let him.

Jesus, restore my Union with you. Restore my soul. Saturate me with your Love; saturate me with your Life.

Linger there for a moment.

Keep on asking, and you will receive what you ask for.
—MATTHEW 7:7 NLT

AM

Begin with settling down. Take a long breath.

As I enter a new day, what do I need to let go of—what is weighing on my heart?

_____

_____

_____

_____

Pause, and give it to God. Let it go.

What do I need from God today?

_____

_____

_____

_____

Pause, and ask for it.

God promises to fill and strengthen you. Receive it.

Jesus, restore my Union with you. I receive your Love. I receive your Life. Strengthen me.

Linger there for a moment.

As we stick with the process, things begin to unfold.

PM

Begin with settling down. Take a long breath.

To enter this afternoon or evening with peace, what do I need to let go of? (Do any worries, fears, or regrets come to mind?)

_____

_____

_____

_____

Pause, and give it to God. Let it go.

At this point in my afternoon or evening, what do I need from God?

_____

_____

_____

_____

Pause, and ask.

God promises to restore your soul. Let him.

Jesus, restore my Union with you. Restore my soul. Saturate me with your Love; saturate me with your Life.

Linger there for a moment.

God is love, and all who live in love live in God.
—1 JOHN 4:16 NLT

AM

Begin with settling down. Take a long breath.

As I enter a new day, what do I need to let go of—what is weighing on my heart?

_____

_____

_____

_____

Pause, and give it to God. Let it go.

What do I need from God today?

_____

_____

_____

_____

Pause, and ask for it.

God promises to fill and strengthen you. Receive it.

Jesus, restore my Union with you. I receive your Love. I receive your Life. Strengthen me.

Linger there for a moment.

It's so simple—to stay in God, stay in a posture of love.

PM

Begin with settling down. Take a long breath.

To enter this afternoon or evening with peace, what do I need to let go of? (Do any worries, fears, or regrets come to mind?)

_____

_____

_____

_____

Pause, and give it to God. Let it go.

At this point in my afternoon or evening, what do I need from God?

_____

_____

_____

_____

Pause, and ask.

God promises to restore your soul. Let him.

Jesus, restore my Union with you. Restore my soul. Saturate me with your Love; saturate me with your Life.

Linger there for a moment.

Come near to God and he will come near to you.

—JAMES 4:8

AM

Begin with settling down. Take a long breath.

As I enter a new day, what do I need to let go of—what is weighing on my heart?

_____

_____

_____

_____

Pause, and give it to God. Let it go.

What do I need from God today?

_____

_____

_____

_____

Pause, and ask for it.

God promises to fill and strengthen you. Receive it.

Jesus, restore my Union with you. I receive your Love. I receive your Life. Strengthen me.

Linger there for a moment.

How is God "coming near" to you today?

PM

Begin with settling down. Take a long breath.

To enter this afternoon or evening with peace, what do I need to let go of? (Do any worries, fears, or regrets come to mind?)

_____

_____

_____

_____

Pause, and give it to God. Let it go.

At this point in my afternoon or evening, what do I need from God?

_____

_____

_____

_____

Pause, and ask.

God promises to restore your soul. Let him.

Jesus, restore my Union with you. Restore my soul. Saturate me with your Love; saturate me with your Life.

Linger there for a moment.

"My grace is sufficient for you."
—2 Corinthians 12:9 NASB

AM

Begin with settling down. Take a long breath.

As I enter a new day, what do I need to let go of—what is weighing on my heart?

_____

_____

_____

_____

Pause, and give it to God. Let it go.

What do I need from God today?

_____

_____

_____

_____

Pause, and ask for it.

God promises to fill and strengthen you. Receive it.

Jesus, restore my Union with you. I receive your Love. I receive your Life. Strengthen me.

Linger there for a moment.

Whatever your current need, there is grace for it.

PM

Begin with settling down. Take a long breath.

To enter this afternoon or evening with peace, what do I need to let go of? (Do any worries, fears, or regrets come to mind?)

_____

_____

_____

_____

Pause, and give it to God. Let it go.

At this point in my afternoon or evening, what do I need from God?

_____

_____

_____

_____

Pause, and ask.

God promises to restore your soul. Let him.

Jesus, restore my Union with you. Restore my soul. Saturate me with your Love; saturate me with your Life.

Linger there for a moment.

May you experience the love of Christ.

—EPHESIANS 3:19 NLT

AM

Begin with settling down. Take a long breath.

As I enter a new day, what do I need to let go of—what is weighing on my heart?

_____

_____

_____

_____

Pause, and give it to God. Let it go.

What do I need from God today?

_____

_____

_____

_____

Pause, and ask for it.

God promises to fill and strengthen you. Receive it.

Jesus, restore my Union with you. I receive your Love. I receive your Life. Strengthen me.

Linger there for a moment.

We are made to experience God's love.

PM

Begin with settling down. Take a long breath.

To enter this afternoon or evening with peace, what do I need to let go of? (Do any worries, fears, or regrets come to mind?)

_____

_____

_____

_____

Pause, and give it to God. Let it go.

At this point in my afternoon or evening, what do I need from God?

_____

_____

_____

_____

Pause, and ask.

God promises to restore your soul. Let him.

Jesus, restore my Union with you. Restore my soul. Saturate me with your Love; saturate me with your Life.

Linger there for a moment.

If you search for him with all your heart
and soul, you will find him.

—DEUTERONOMY 4:29 NLT

AM

Begin with settling down. Take a long breath.

As I enter a new day, what do I need to let go of—what is weighing on
my heart?

_____

_____

_____

_____

Pause, and give it to God. Let it go.

What do I need from God today?

_____

_____

_____

_____

Pause, and ask for it.

God promises to fill and strengthen you. Receive it.

Jesus, restore my Union with you. I receive your Love. I receive your
Life. Strengthen me.

Linger there for a moment.

Don't let the Pause become work; use it to find God!

PM

Begin with settling down. Take a long breath.

To enter this afternoon or evening with peace, what do I need to let go of? (Do any worries, fears, or regrets come to mind?)

_____

_____

_____

_____

Pause, and give it to God. Let it go.

At this point in my afternoon or evening, what do I need from God?

_____

_____

_____

_____

Pause, and ask.

God promises to restore your soul. Let him.

Jesus, restore my Union with you. Restore my soul. Saturate me with your Love; saturate me with your Life.

Linger there for a moment.

Whoever wants to save their life will lose it, but
whoever loses their life for me will find it.
—MATTHEW 16:25

AM

Begin with settling down. Take a long breath.

As I enter a new day, what do I need to let go of—what is weighing on
my heart?

_____

_____

_____

_____

Pause, and give it to God. Let it go.

What do I need from God today?

_____

_____

_____

_____

Pause, and ask for it.

God promises to fill and strengthen you. Receive it.

Jesus, restore my Union with you. I receive your Love. I receive your
Life. Strengthen me.

Linger there for a moment.

The beauty of surrender is that it
removes so much pressure.

PM

Begin with settling down. Take a long breath.

To enter this afternoon or evening with peace, what do I need to let go
of? (Do any worries, fears, or regrets come to mind?)

_____

_____

_____

_____

Pause, and give it to God. Let it go.

At this point in my afternoon or evening, what do I need from God?

_____

_____

_____

_____

Pause, and ask.

God promises to restore your soul. Let him.

Jesus, restore my Union with you. Restore my soul. Saturate me with
your Love; saturate me with your Life.

Linger there for a moment.

We love, because He first loved us.

—1 JOHN 4:19 NASB

AM

Begin with settling down. Take a long breath.

As I enter a new day, what do I need to let go of—what is weighing on my heart?

_____

_____

_____

_____

Pause, and give it to God. Let it go.

What do I need from God today?

_____

_____

_____

_____

Pause, and ask for it.

God promises to fill and strengthen you. Receive it.

Jesus, restore my Union with you. I receive your Love. I receive your Life. Strengthen me.

Linger there for a moment.

Even loving well can become pressure.
Let Christ fill you first.

PM

Begin with settling down. Take a long breath.

To enter this afternoon or evening with peace, what do I need to let go of? (Do any worries, fears, or regrets come to mind?)

_____

_____

_____

_____

Pause, and give it to God. Let it go.

At this point in my afternoon or evening, what do I need from God?

_____

_____

_____

_____

Pause, and ask.

God promises to restore your soul. Let him.

Jesus, restore my Union with you. Restore my soul. Saturate me with your Love; saturate me with your Life.

Linger there for a moment.

The joy of GOD is your strength!
—NEHEMIAH 8:10 THE MESSAGE

AM

Begin with settling down. Take a long breath.

As I enter a new day, what do I need to let go of—what is weighing on
my heart?

_____

_____

_____

_____

Pause, and give it to God. Let it go.

What do I need from God today?

_____

_____

_____

_____

Pause, and ask for it.

God promises to fill and strengthen you. Receive it.

Jesus, restore my Union with you. I receive your Love. I receive your
Life. Strengthen me.

Linger there for a moment.

Ask God to fill you with his joy today!

PM

Begin with settling down. Take a long breath.

To enter this afternoon or evening with peace, what do I need to let go of? (Do any worries, fears, or regrets come to mind?)

_____

_____

_____

_____

Pause, and give it to God. Let it go.

At this point in my afternoon or evening, what do I need from God?

_____

_____

_____

_____

Pause, and ask.

God promises to restore your soul. Let him.

Jesus, restore my Union with you. Restore my soul. Saturate me with your Love; saturate me with your Life.

Linger there for a moment.

Three things will last forever—faith, hope, and love.
—1 Corinthians 13:13 nlt

AM

Begin with settling down. Take a long breath.

As I enter a new day, what do I need to let go of—what is weighing on my heart?

_____

_____

_____

_____

Pause, and give it to God. Let it go.

What do I need from God today?

_____

_____

_____

_____

Pause, and ask for it.

God promises to fill and strengthen you. Receive it.

Jesus, restore my Union with you. I receive your Love. I receive your Life. Strengthen me.

Linger there for a moment.

First things first—your faith, hope, and love.

PM

Begin with settling down. Take a long breath.

To enter this afternoon or evening with peace, what do I need to let go of? (Do any worries, fears, or regrets come to mind?)

_____

_____

_____

_____

Pause, and give it to God. Let it go.

At this point in my afternoon or evening, what do I need from God?

_____

_____

_____

_____

Pause, and ask.

God promises to restore your soul. Let him.

Jesus, restore my Union with you. Restore my soul. Saturate me with your Love; saturate me with your Life.

Linger there for a moment.

Enter through the narrow gate. For wide is the gate
and broad is the road that leads to destruction.
—MATTHEW 7:13

AM

Begin with settling down. Take a long breath.

As I enter a new day, what do I need to let go of—what is weighing on
my heart?

_____

_____

_____

_____

Pause, and give it to God. Let it go.

What do I need from God today?

_____

_____

_____

_____

Pause, and ask for it.

God promises to fill and strengthen you. Receive it.

Jesus, restore my Union with you. I receive your Love. I receive your
Life. Strengthen me.

Linger there for a moment.

Remember—the world is not the friend of your soul.

PM

Begin with settling down. Take a long breath.

To enter this afternoon or evening with peace, what do I need to let go of? (Do any worries, fears, or regrets come to mind?)

_____

_____

_____

_____

Pause, and give it to God. Let it go.

At this point in my afternoon or evening, what do I need from God?

_____

_____

_____

_____

Pause, and ask.

God promises to restore your soul. Let him.

Jesus, restore my Union with you. Restore my soul. Saturate me with your Love; saturate me with your Life.

Linger there for a moment.

We know how dearly God loves us, because he has
given us the Holy Spirit to fill our hearts with his love.
—ROMANS 5:5 NLT

AM

Begin with settling down. Take a long breath.

As I enter a new day, what do I need to let go of—what is weighing on
my heart?

_____

_____

_____

_____

Pause, and give it to God. Let it go.

What do I need from God today?

_____

_____

_____

_____

Pause, and ask for it.

God promises to fill and strengthen you. Receive it.

Jesus, restore my Union with you. I receive your Love. I receive your
Life. Strengthen me.

Linger there for a moment.

O Holy Spirit—fill my heart afresh with your love today.

PM

Begin with settling down. Take a long breath.

To enter this afternoon or evening with peace, what do I need to let go of? (Do any worries, fears, or regrets come to mind?)

_____

_____

_____

_____

Pause, and give it to God. Let it go.

At this point in my afternoon or evening, what do I need from God?

_____

_____

_____

_____

Pause, and ask.

God promises to restore your soul. Let him.

Jesus, restore my Union with you. Restore my soul. Saturate me with your Love; saturate me with your Life.

Linger there for a moment.

I pray that God, the source of hope, will fill you
completely with joy and peace because you trust in him.
—ROMANS 15:13 NLT

AM

Begin with settling down. Take a long breath.

As I enter a new day, what do I need to let go of—what is weighing on
my heart?

_____

_____

_____

_____

Pause, and give it to God. Let it go.

What do I need from God today?

_____

_____

_____

_____

Pause, and ask for it.

God promises to fill and strengthen you. Receive it.

Jesus, restore my Union with you. I receive your Love. I receive your
Life. Strengthen me.

Linger there for a moment.

I do trust you, God. My emotions waver, but I trust you.

PM

Begin with settling down. Take a long breath.

To enter this afternoon or evening with peace, what do I need to let go of? (Do any worries, fears, or regrets come to mind?)

_____

_____

_____

_____

Pause, and give it to God. Let it go.

At this point in my afternoon or evening, what do I need from God?

_____

_____

_____

_____

Pause, and ask.

God promises to restore your soul. Let him.

Jesus, restore my Union with you. Restore my soul. Saturate me with your Love; saturate me with your Life.

Linger there for a moment.

Who is it that overcomes the world? Only the
one who believes that Jesus is the Son of God.
—1 JOHN 5:5

AM

Begin with settling down. Take a long breath.

As I enter a new day, what do I need to let go of—what is weighing on
my heart?

_____

_____

_____

_____

Pause, and give it to God. Let it go.

What do I need from God today?

_____

_____

_____

_____

Pause, and ask for it.

God promises to fill and strengthen you. Receive it.

Jesus, restore my Union with you. I receive your Love. I receive your
Life. Strengthen me.

Linger there for a moment.

I reject the madness of this world. I belong to God!

PM

Begin with settling down. Take a long breath.

To enter this afternoon or evening with peace, what do I need to let go of? (Do any worries, fears, or regrets come to mind?)

_____

_____

_____

_____

Pause, and give it to God. Let it go.

At this point in my afternoon or evening, what do I need from God?

_____

_____

_____

_____

Pause, and ask.

God promises to restore your soul. Let him.

Jesus, restore my Union with you. Restore my soul. Saturate me with your Love; saturate me with your Life.

Linger there for a moment.

I can do all things through Christ who strengthens me.
—PHILIPPIANS 4:13 NKJV

AM

Begin with settling down. Take a long breath.

As I enter a new day, what do I need to let go of—what is weighing on my heart?

_____

_____

_____

_____

Pause, and give it to God. Let it go.

What do I need from God today?

_____

_____

_____

_____

Pause, and ask for it.

God promises to fill and strengthen you. Receive it.

Jesus, restore my Union with you. I receive your Love. I receive your Life. Strengthen me.

Linger there for a moment.

You are my strength today, Jesus.

PM

Begin with settling down. Take a long breath.

To enter this afternoon or evening with peace, what do I need to let go of? (Do any worries, fears, or regrets come to mind?)

_____

_____

_____

_____

Pause, and give it to God. Let it go.

At this point in my afternoon or evening, what do I need from God?

_____

_____

_____

_____

Pause, and ask.

God promises to restore your soul. Let him.

Jesus, restore my Union with you. Restore my soul. Saturate me with your Love; saturate me with your Life.

Linger there for a moment.

Trust in the LORD with all your heart and
lean not on your own understanding.
—PROVERBS 3:5

AM

Begin with settling down. Take a long breath.

As I enter a new day, what do I need to let go of—what is weighing on
my heart?

_____

_____

_____

_____

Pause, and give it to God. Let it go.

What do I need from God today?

_____

_____

_____

_____

Pause, and ask for it.

God promises to fill and strengthen you. Receive it.

Jesus, restore my Union with you. I receive your Love. I receive your
Life. Strengthen me.

Linger there for a moment.

I don't need understanding, Lord. I need you!

PM

Begin with settling down. Take a long breath.

To enter this afternoon or evening with peace, what do I need to let go of? (Do any worries, fears, or regrets come to mind?)

_____

_____

_____

_____

Pause, and give it to God. Let it go.

At this point in my afternoon or evening, what do I need from God?

_____

_____

_____

_____

Pause, and ask.

God promises to restore your soul. Let him.

Jesus, restore my Union with you. Restore my soul. Saturate me with your Love; saturate me with your Life.

Linger there for a moment.

Guard against corruption from the godless world.
—JAMES 1:27 THE MESSAGE

AM

Begin with settling down. Take a long breath.

As I enter a new day, what do I need to let go of—what is weighing on my heart?

_____

_____

_____

_____

Pause, and give it to God. Let it go.

What do I need from God today?

_____

_____

_____

_____

Pause, and ask for it.

God promises to fill and strengthen you. Receive it.

Jesus, restore my Union with you. I receive your Love. I receive your Life. Strengthen me.

Linger there for a moment.

I pause to pull away from the crazy-making world.

PM

Begin with settling down. Take a long breath.

To enter this afternoon or evening with peace, what do I need to let go of? (Do any worries, fears, or regrets come to mind?)

_____

_____

_____

_____

Pause, and give it to God. Let it go.

At this point in my afternoon or evening, what do I need from God?

_____

_____

_____

_____

Pause, and ask.

God promises to restore your soul. Let him.

Jesus, restore my Union with you. Restore my soul. Saturate me with your Love; saturate me with your Life.

Linger there for a moment.

For nothing will be impossible with God.
—LUKE 1:37 ESV

AM

Begin with settling down. Take a long breath.

As I enter a new day, what do I need to let go of—what is weighing on my heart?

_____

_____

_____

_____

Pause, and give it to God. Let it go.

What do I need from God today?

_____

_____

_____

_____

Pause, and ask for it.

God promises to fill and strengthen you. Receive it.

Jesus, restore my Union with you. I receive your Love. I receive your Life. Strengthen me.

Linger there for a moment.

I turn it all over to you again, Father.

PM

Begin with settling down. Take a long breath.

To enter this afternoon or evening with peace, what do I need to let go of? (Do any worries, fears, or regrets come to mind?)

_____

_____

_____

_____

Pause, and give it to God. Let it go.

At this point in my afternoon or evening, what do I need from God?

_____

_____

_____

_____

Pause, and ask.

God promises to restore your soul. Let him.

Jesus, restore my Union with you. Restore my soul. Saturate me with your Love; saturate me with your Life.

Linger there for a moment.

He gives strength to the weary and
increases the power of the weak.
—ISAIAH 40:29

AM

Begin with settling down. Take a long breath.

As I enter a new day, what do I need to let go of—what is weighing on
my heart?

_____

_____

_____

_____

Pause, and give it to God. Let it go.

What do I need from God today?

_____

_____

_____

_____

Pause, and ask for it.

God promises to fill and strengthen you. Receive it.

Jesus, restore my Union with you. I receive your Love. I receive your
Life. Strengthen me.

Linger there for a moment.

I need your strength, Lord. Strengthen me.

PM

Begin with settling down. Take a long breath.

To enter this afternoon or evening with peace, what do I need to let go of? (Do any worries, fears, or regrets come to mind?)

_____

_____

_____

_____

Pause, and give it to God. Let it go.

At this point in my afternoon or evening, what do I need from God?

_____

_____

_____

_____

Pause, and ask.

God promises to restore your soul. Let him.

Jesus, restore my Union with you. Restore my soul. Saturate me with your Love; saturate me with your Life.

Linger there for a moment.

The LORD is close to the brokenhearted;
he rescues those whose spirits are crushed.
—PSALM 34:18 NLT

AM

Begin with settling down. Take a long breath.

As I enter a new day, what do I need to let go of—what is weighing on my heart?

_____

_____

_____

_____

Pause, and give it to God. Let it go.

What do I need from God today?

_____

_____

_____

_____

Pause, and ask for it.

God promises to fill and strengthen you. Receive it.

Jesus, restore my Union with you. I receive your Love. I receive your Life. Strengthen me.

Linger there for a moment.

When the pressure is on, Jesus is right there with you.

PM

Begin with settling down. Take a long breath.

To enter this afternoon or evening with peace, what do I need to let go of? (Do any worries, fears, or regrets come to mind?)

_____

_____

_____

_____

Pause, and give it to God. Let it go.

At this point in my afternoon or evening, what do I need from God?

_____

_____

_____

_____

Pause, and ask.

God promises to restore your soul. Let him.

Jesus, restore my Union with you. Restore my soul. Saturate me with your Love; saturate me with your Life.

Linger there for a moment.

And we know that in all things God works
for the good of those who love him.
—ROMANS 8:28

AM

Begin with settling down. Take a long breath.

As I enter a new day, what do I need to let go of—what is weighing on
my heart?

_____

_____

_____

_____

Pause, and give it to God. Let it go.

What do I need from God today?

_____

_____

_____

_____

Pause, and ask for it.

God promises to fill and strengthen you. Receive it.

Jesus, restore my Union with you. I receive your Love. I receive your
Life. Strengthen me.

Linger there for a moment.

You are working on my behalf right now, Jesus.

PM

Begin with settling down. Take a long breath.

To enter this afternoon or evening with peace, what do I need to let go of? (Do any worries, fears, or regrets come to mind?)

_____

_____

_____

_____

Pause, and give it to God. Let it go.

At this point in my afternoon or evening, what do I need from God?

_____

_____

_____

_____

Pause, and ask.

God promises to restore your soul. Let him.

Jesus, restore my Union with you. Restore my soul. Saturate me with your Love; saturate me with your Life.

Linger there for a moment.

But blessed is the one who trusts in the
LORD, whose confidence is in him.
—JEREMIAH 17:7

AM

Begin with settling down. Take a long breath.

As I enter a new day, what do I need to let go of—what is weighing on
my heart?

_____

_____

_____

_____

Pause, and give it to God. Let it go.

What do I need from God today?

_____

_____

_____

_____

Pause, and ask for it.

God promises to fill and strengthen you. Receive it.

Jesus, restore my Union with you. I receive your Love. I receive your
Life. Strengthen me.

Linger there for a moment.

I choose to put my confidence in nothing but you, God.

PM

Begin with settling down. Take a long breath.

To enter this afternoon or evening with peace, what do I need to let go of? (Do any worries, fears, or regrets come to mind?)

_____

_____

_____

_____

Pause, and give it to God. Let it go.

At this point in my afternoon or evening, what do I need from God?

_____

_____

_____

_____

Pause, and ask.

God promises to restore your soul. Let him.

Jesus, restore my Union with you. Restore my soul. Saturate me with your Love; saturate me with your Life.

Linger there for a moment.

If you remain in my word, then
you are truly my disciples.
—JOHN 8:31 WEB

AM

Begin with settling down. Take a long breath.

As I enter a new day, what do I need to let go of—what is weighing on my heart?

_____

_____

_____

_____

Pause, and give it to God. Let it go.

What do I need from God today?

_____

_____

_____

_____

Pause, and ask for it.

God promises to fill and strengthen you. Receive it.

Jesus, restore my Union with you. I receive your Love. I receive your Life. Strengthen me.

Linger there for a moment.

I pause and give you my attention, Lord.

PM

Begin with settling down. Take a long breath.

To enter this afternoon or evening with peace, what do I need to let go of? (Do any worries, fears, or regrets come to mind?)

_____

_____

_____

_____

Pause, and give it to God. Let it go.

At this point in my afternoon or evening, what do I need from God?

_____

_____

_____

_____

Pause, and ask.

God promises to restore your soul. Let him.

Jesus, restore my Union with you. Restore my soul. Saturate me with your Love; saturate me with your Life.

Linger there for a moment.

Praise be to the LORD, to God our Savior,
who daily bears our burdens.
—PSALM 68:19

AM

Begin with settling down. Take a long breath.

As I enter a new day, what do I need to let go of—what is weighing on
my heart?

_____

_____

_____

_____

Pause, and give it to God. Let it go.

What do I need from God today?

_____

_____

_____

_____

Pause, and ask for it.

God promises to fill and strengthen you. Receive it.

Jesus, restore my Union with you. I receive your Love. I receive your
Life. Strengthen me.

Linger there for a moment.

I stop and give my burdens to you, Father.

PM

Begin with settling down. Take a long breath.

To enter this afternoon or evening with peace, what do I need to let go of? (Do any worries, fears, or regrets come to mind?)

_____

_____

_____

_____

Pause, and give it to God. Let it go.

At this point in my afternoon or evening, what do I need from God?

_____

_____

_____

_____

Pause, and ask.

God promises to restore your soul. Let him.

Jesus, restore my Union with you. Restore my soul. Saturate me with your Love; saturate me with your Life.

Linger there for a moment.

If God is for us, who can be against us?
—ROMANS 8:31

AM

Begin with settling down. Take a long breath.

As I enter a new day, what do I need to let go of—what is weighing on my heart?

_____

_____

_____

_____

Pause, and give it to God. Let it go.

What do I need from God today?

_____

_____

_____

_____

Pause, and ask for it.

God promises to fill and strengthen you. Receive it.

Jesus, restore my Union with you. I receive your Love. I receive your Life. Strengthen me.

Linger there for a moment.

Life can be rough, but God is on your side.

PM

Begin with settling down. Take a long breath.

To enter this afternoon or evening with peace, what do I need to let go of? (Do any worries, fears, or regrets come to mind?)

_____

_____

_____

_____

Pause, and give it to God. Let it go.

At this point in my afternoon or evening, what do I need from God?

_____

_____

_____

_____

Pause, and ask.

God promises to restore your soul. Let him.

Jesus, restore my Union with you. Restore my soul. Saturate me with your Love; saturate me with your Life.

Linger there for a moment.

Can any one of you by worrying add
a single hour to your life?
—MATTHEW 6:27

AM

Begin with settling down. Take a long breath.

As I enter a new day, what do I need to let go of—what is weighing on
my heart?

_____

_____

_____

_____

Pause, and give it to God. Let it go.

What do I need from God today?

_____

_____

_____

_____

Pause, and ask for it.

God promises to fill and strengthen you. Receive it.

Jesus, restore my Union with you. I receive your Love. I receive your
Life. Strengthen me.

Linger there for a moment.

Worry is a soul-killer. Push it back!

PM

Begin with settling down. Take a long breath.

To enter this afternoon or evening with peace, what do I need to let go of? (Do any worries, fears, or regrets come to mind?)

_____

_____

_____

_____

Pause, and give it to God. Let it go.

At this point in my afternoon or evening, what do I need from God?

_____

_____

_____

_____

Pause, and ask.

God promises to restore your soul. Let him.

Jesus, restore my Union with you. Restore my soul. Saturate me with your Love; saturate me with your Life.

Linger there for a moment.

I sought the LORD, and he answered me;
he delivered me from all my fears.
—PSALM 34:4

AM

Begin with settling down. Take a long breath.

As I enter a new day, what do I need to let go of—what is weighing on my heart?

_____

_____

_____

_____

Pause, and give it to God. Let it go.

What do I need from God today?

_____

_____

_____

_____

Pause, and ask for it.

God promises to fill and strengthen you. Receive it.

Jesus, restore my Union with you. I receive your Love. I receive your Life. Strengthen me.

Linger there for a moment.

I pause to seek you again, God. Deliver me.

PM

Begin with settling down. Take a long breath.

To enter this afternoon or evening with peace, what do I need to let go of? (Do any worries, fears, or regrets come to mind?)

_____

_____

_____

_____

Pause, and give it to God. Let it go.

At this point in my afternoon or evening, what do I need from God?

_____

_____

_____

_____

Pause, and ask.

God promises to restore your soul. Let him.

Jesus, restore my Union with you. Restore my soul. Saturate me with your Love; saturate me with your Life.

Linger there for a moment.

Surely I am with you always, to the very end of the age.
—MATTHEW 28:20

AM

Begin with settling down. Take a long breath.

As I enter a new day, what do I need to let go of—what is weighing on my heart?

_____

_____

_____

_____

Pause, and give it to God. Let it go.

What do I need from God today?

_____

_____

_____

_____

Pause, and ask for it.

God promises to fill and strengthen you. Receive it.

Jesus, restore my Union with you. I receive your Love. I receive your Life. Strengthen me.

Linger there for a moment.

You are never alone, never on your own.

PM

Begin with settling down. Take a long breath.

To enter this afternoon or evening with peace, what do I need to let go of? (Do any worries, fears, or regrets come to mind?)

_____

_____

_____

_____

Pause, and give it to God. Let it go.

At this point in my afternoon or evening, what do I need from God?

_____

_____

_____

Pause, and ask.

God promises to restore your soul. Let him.

Jesus, restore my Union with you. Restore my soul. Saturate me with your Love; saturate me with your Life.

Linger there for a moment.

Anxiety weighs down the heart, but
a kind word cheers it up.
—PROVERBS 12:25

AM

Begin with settling down. Take a long breath.

As I enter a new day, what do I need to let go of—what is weighing on my heart?

_____

_____

_____

_____

Pause, and give it to God. Let it go.

What do I need from God today?

_____

_____

_____

_____

Pause, and ask for it.

God promises to fill and strengthen you. Receive it.

Jesus, restore my Union with you. I receive your Love. I receive your Life. Strengthen me.

Linger there for a moment.

I give it all to you, Lord. Lift my heart today.

PM

Begin with settling down. Take a long breath.

To enter this afternoon or evening with peace, what do I need to let go of? (Do any worries, fears, or regrets come to mind?)

_____

_____

_____

_____

Pause, and give it to God. Let it go.

At this point in my afternoon or evening, what do I need from God?

_____

_____

_____

_____

Pause, and ask.

God promises to restore your soul. Let him.

Jesus, restore my Union with you. Restore my soul. Saturate me with your Love; saturate me with your Life.

Linger there for a moment.

When I am afraid, I put my trust in you.

—PSALM 56:3

AM

Begin with settling down. Take a long breath.

As I enter a new day, what do I need to let go of—what is weighing on my heart?

_____

_____

_____

_____

Pause, and give it to God. Let it go.

What do I need from God today?

_____

_____

_____

_____

Pause, and ask for it.

God promises to fill and strengthen you. Receive it.

Jesus, restore my Union with you. I receive your Love. I receive your Life. Strengthen me.

Linger there for a moment.

We choose to trust; emotions follow after.

PM

Begin with settling down. Take a long breath.

To enter this afternoon or evening with peace, what do I need to let go of? (Do any worries, fears, or regrets come to mind?)

_____

_____

_____

_____

Pause, and give it to God. Let it go.

At this point in my afternoon or evening, what do I need from God?

_____

_____

_____

_____

Pause, and ask.

God promises to restore your soul. Let him.

Jesus, restore my Union with you. Restore my soul. Saturate me with your Love; saturate me with your Life.

Linger there for a moment.

In repentance and rest is your salvation, in
quietness and trust is your strength.
—Isaiah 30:15

AM

Begin with settling down. Take a long breath.

As I enter a new day, what do I need to let go of—what is weighing on
my heart?

_____

_____

_____

_____

Pause, and give it to God. Let it go.

What do I need from God today?

_____

_____

_____

_____

Pause, and ask for it.

God promises to fill and strengthen you. Receive it.

Jesus, restore my Union with you. I receive your Love. I receive your
Life. Strengthen me.

Linger there for a moment.

All you need to do right now is get
quiet for a few moments.

PM

Begin with settling down. Take a long breath.

To enter this afternoon or evening with peace, what do I need to let go
of? (Do any worries, fears, or regrets come to mind?)

_____

_____

_____

_____

Pause, and give it to God. Let it go.

At this point in my afternoon or evening, what do I need from God?

_____

_____

_____

_____

Pause, and ask.

God promises to restore your soul. Let him.

Jesus, restore my Union with you. Restore my soul. Saturate me with
your Love; saturate me with your Life.

Linger there for a moment.

I am the vine; you are the branches.
—John 15:5

AM

Begin with settling down. Take a long breath.

As I enter a new day, what do I need to let go of—what is weighing on my heart?

_____

_____

_____

_____

Pause, and give it to God. Let it go.

What do I need from God today?

_____

_____

_____

_____

Pause, and ask for it.

God promises to fill and strengthen you. Receive it.

Jesus, restore my Union with you. I receive your Love. I receive your Life. Strengthen me.

Linger there for a moment.

Your life is an extension of the life of Jesus.

PM

Begin with settling down. Take a long breath.

To enter this afternoon or evening with peace, what do I need to let go of? (Do any worries, fears, or regrets come to mind?)

_____

_____

_____

_____

Pause, and give it to God. Let it go.

At this point in my afternoon or evening, what do I need from God?

_____

_____

_____

_____

Pause, and ask.

God promises to restore your soul. Let him.

Jesus, restore my Union with you. Restore my soul. Saturate me with your Love; saturate me with your Life.

Linger there for a moment.

Never will I leave you; never will I forsake you.
—Hebrews 13:5

AM

Begin with settling down. Take a long breath.

As I enter a new day, what do I need to let go of—what is weighing on my heart?

_____

_____

_____

_____

Pause, and give it to God. Let it go.

What do I need from God today?

_____

_____

_____

_____

Pause, and ask for it.

God promises to fill and strengthen you. Receive it.

Jesus, restore my Union with you. I receive your Love. I receive your Life. Strengthen me.

Linger there for a moment.

God is right here, at your side.

PM

Begin with settling down. Take a long breath.

To enter this afternoon or evening with peace, what do I need to let go of? (Do any worries, fears, or regrets come to mind?)

_____

_____

_____

_____

Pause, and give it to God. Let it go.

At this point in my afternoon or evening, what do I need from God?

_____

_____

_____

_____

Pause, and ask.

God promises to restore your soul. Let him.

Jesus, restore my Union with you. Restore my soul. Saturate me with your Love; saturate me with your Life.

Linger there for a moment.

Commit your way to the LORD; trust
in him and he will do this.
—PSALM 37:5

AM

Begin with settling down. Take a long breath.

As I enter a new day, what do I need to let go of—what is weighing on
my heart?

_____

_____

_____

_____

Pause, and give it to God. Let it go.

What do I need from God today?

_____

_____

_____

_____

Pause, and ask for it.

God promises to fill and strengthen you. Receive it.

Jesus, restore my Union with you. I receive your Love. I receive your
Life. Strengthen me.

Linger there for a moment.

Give all your plans to God; don't carry them.

PM

Begin with settling down. Take a long breath.

To enter this afternoon or evening with peace, what do I need to let go of? (Do any worries, fears, or regrets come to mind?)

_____

_____

_____

_____

Pause, and give it to God. Let it go.

At this point in my afternoon or evening, what do I need from God?

_____

_____

_____

_____

Pause, and ask.

God promises to restore your soul. Let him.

Jesus, restore my Union with you. Restore my soul. Saturate me with your Love; saturate me with your Life.

Linger there for a moment.

We have peace with God through our Lord Jesus Christ.
—ROMANS 5:1

AM

Begin with settling down. Take a long breath.

As I enter a new day, what do I need to let go of—what is weighing on my heart?

_____

_____

_____

_____

Pause, and give it to God. Let it go.

What do I need from God today?

_____

_____

_____

_____

Pause, and ask for it.

God promises to fill and strengthen you. Receive it.

Jesus, restore my Union with you. I receive your Love. I receive your Life. Strengthen me.

Linger there for a moment.

Jesus—I receive this peace.

PM

Begin with settling down. Take a long breath.

To enter this afternoon or evening with peace, what do I need to let go of? (Do any worries, fears, or regrets come to mind?)

_____

_____

_____

_____

Pause, and give it to God. Let it go.

At this point in my afternoon or evening, what do I need from God?

_____

_____

_____

_____

Pause, and ask.

God promises to restore your soul. Let him.

Jesus, restore my Union with you. Restore my soul. Saturate me with your Love; saturate me with your Life.

Linger there for a moment.

"Love the Lord your God with all your heart and
with all your soul and with all your mind."
—MATTHEW 22:37–38

AM

Begin with settling down. Take a long breath.

As I enter a new day, what do I need to let go of—what is weighing on
my heart?

_____

_____

_____

_____

Pause, and give it to God. Let it go.

What do I need from God today?

_____

_____

_____

_____

Pause, and ask for it.

God promises to fill and strengthen you. Receive it.

Jesus, restore my Union with you. I receive your Love. I receive your
Life. Strengthen me.

Linger there for a moment.

As you choose love, you choose to align with God.

PM

Begin with settling down. Take a long breath.

To enter this afternoon or evening with peace, what do I need to let go of? (Do any worries, fears, or regrets come to mind?)

_____

_____

_____

_____

Pause, and give it to God. Let it go.

At this point in my afternoon or evening, what do I need from God?

_____

_____

_____

_____

Pause, and ask.

God promises to restore your soul. Let him.

Jesus, restore my Union with you. Restore my soul. Saturate me with your Love; saturate me with your Life.

Linger there for a moment.

Love your neighbor as yourself.

—MATTHEW 22:39

AM

Begin with settling down. Take a long breath.

As I enter a new day, what do I need to let go of—what is weighing on my heart?

_____

_____

_____

_____

Pause, and give it to God. Let it go.

What do I need from God today?

_____

_____

_____

_____

Pause, and ask for it.

God promises to fill and strengthen you. Receive it.

Jesus, restore my Union with you. I receive your Love. I receive your Life. Strengthen me.

Linger there for a moment.

Love actually helps us release people to God.

PM

Begin with settling down. Take a long breath.

To enter this afternoon or evening with peace, what do I need to let go of? (Do any worries, fears, or regrets come to mind?)

_____

_____

_____

_____

Pause, and give it to God. Let it go.

At this point in my afternoon or evening, what do I need from God?

_____

_____

_____

_____

Pause, and ask.

God promises to restore your soul. Let him.

Jesus, restore my Union with you. Restore my soul. Saturate me with your Love; saturate me with your Life.

Linger there for a moment.

The world has been crucified to me, and I to the world.
—GALATIANS 6:14

AM

Begin with settling down. Take a long breath.

As I enter a new day, what do I need to let go of—what is weighing on my heart?

_____

_____

_____

_____

Pause, and give it to God. Let it go.

What do I need from God today?

_____

_____

_____

_____

Pause, and ask for it.

God promises to fill and strengthen you. Receive it.

Jesus, restore my Union with you. I receive your Love. I receive your Life. Strengthen me.

Linger there for a moment.

The cross is your rescue. You don't have
to dwell in the toxic anymore.

PM

Begin with settling down. Take a long breath.

To enter this afternoon or evening with peace, what do I need to let go
of? (Do any worries, fears, or regrets come to mind?)

_____

_____

_____

_____

Pause, and give it to God. Let it go.

At this point in my afternoon or evening, what do I need from God?

_____

_____

_____

_____

Pause, and ask.

God promises to restore your soul. Let him.

Jesus, restore my Union with you. Restore my soul. Saturate me with
your Love; saturate me with your Life.

Linger there for a moment.

Anyone who intends to come with me has to let me lead.
—Luke 9:23 The Message

AM

Begin with settling down. Take a long breath.

As I enter a new day, what do I need to let go of—what is weighing on my heart?

_____

_____

_____

_____

Pause, and give it to God. Let it go.

What do I need from God today?

_____

_____

_____

_____

Pause, and ask for it.

God promises to fill and strengthen you. Receive it.

Jesus, restore my Union with you. I receive your Love. I receive your Life. Strengthen me.

Linger there for a moment.

We pause to listen and let God be our guide.

PM

Begin with settling down. Take a long breath.

To enter this afternoon or evening with peace, what do I need to let go of? (Do any worries, fears, or regrets come to mind?)

_____

_____

_____

_____

Pause, and give it to God. Let it go.

At this point in my afternoon or evening, what do I need from God?

_____

_____

_____

_____

Pause, and ask.

God promises to restore your soul. Let him.

Jesus, restore my Union with you. Restore my soul. Saturate me with your Love; saturate me with your Life.

Linger there for a moment.

When Christ, who is your life, appears, then
you also will appear with him in glory.
—COLOSSIANS 3:4

AM

Begin with settling down. Take a long breath.

As I enter a new day, what do I need to let go of—what is weighing on
my heart?

_____

_____

_____

_____

Pause, and give it to God. Let it go.

What do I need from God today?

_____

_____

_____

_____

Pause, and ask for it.

God promises to fill and strengthen you. Receive it.

Jesus, restore my Union with you. I receive your Love. I receive your
Life. Strengthen me.

Linger there for a moment.

If you give your life to Jesus, then
Jesus truly becomes your life.

PM

Begin with settling down. Take a long breath.

To enter this afternoon or evening with peace, what do I need to let go of? (Do any worries, fears, or regrets come to mind?)

_____

_____

_____

_____

Pause, and give it to God. Let it go.

At this point in my afternoon or evening, what do I need from God?

_____

_____

_____

_____

Pause, and ask.

God promises to restore your soul. Let him.

Jesus, restore my Union with you. Restore my soul. Saturate me with your Love; saturate me with your Life.

Linger there for a moment.

He goes on ahead of them, and his sheep
follow him because they know his voice.
—JOHN 10:4

AM

Begin with settling down. Take a long breath.

As I enter a new day, what do I need to let go of—what is weighing on
my heart?

_____

_____

_____

_____

Pause, and give it to God. Let it go.

What do I need from God today?

_____

_____

_____

_____

Pause, and ask for it.

God promises to fill and strengthen you. Receive it.

Jesus, restore my Union with you. I receive your Love. I receive your
Life. Strengthen me.

Linger there for a moment.

Will you follow God or just go your way into each day?

PM

Begin with settling down. Take a long breath.

To enter this afternoon or evening with peace, what do I need to let go of? (Do any worries, fears, or regrets come to mind?)

_____

_____

_____

_____

Pause, and give it to God. Let it go.

At this point in my afternoon or evening, what do I need from God?

_____

_____

_____

_____

Pause, and ask.

God promises to restore your soul. Let him.

Jesus, restore my Union with you. Restore my soul. Saturate me with your Love; saturate me with your Life.

Linger there for a moment.

> Why am I discouraged? Why is my heart
> so sad? I will put my hope in God!
> —Psalm 42:5 nlt

AM

Begin with settling down. Take a long breath.

As I enter a new day, what do I need to let go of—what is weighing on my heart?

_____

_____

_____

_____

Pause, and give it to God. Let it go.

What do I need from God today?

_____

_____

_____

_____

Pause, and ask for it.

God promises to fill and strengthen you. Receive it.

Jesus, restore my Union with you. I receive your Love. I receive your Life. Strengthen me.

Linger there for a moment.

Where is the hope of your soul placed right now?

PM

Begin with settling down. Take a long breath.

To enter this afternoon or evening with peace, what do I need to let go of? (Do any worries, fears, or regrets come to mind?)

_____

_____

_____

_____

Pause, and give it to God. Let it go.

At this point in my afternoon or evening, what do I need from God?

_____

_____

_____

_____

Pause, and ask.

God promises to restore your soul. Let him.

Jesus, restore my Union with you. Restore my soul. Saturate me with your Love; saturate me with your Life.

Linger there for a moment.

The LORD himself will fight for you.

—EXODUS 14:14 NLT

AM

Begin with settling down. Take a long breath.

As I enter a new day, what do I need to let go of—what is weighing on my heart?

_____

_____

_____

_____

Pause, and give it to God. Let it go.

What do I need from God today?

_____

_____

_____

_____

Pause, and ask for it.

God promises to fill and strengthen you. Receive it.

Jesus, restore my Union with you. I receive your Love. I receive your Life. Strengthen me.

Linger there for a moment.

Your God is a warrior because there are
things in life worth fighting for.

PM

Begin with settling down. Take a long breath.

To enter this afternoon or evening with peace, what do I need to let go
of? (Do any worries, fears, or regrets come to mind?)

_____

_____

_____

_____

Pause, and give it to God. Let it go.

At this point in my afternoon or evening, what do I need from God?

_____

_____

_____

_____

Pause, and ask.

God promises to restore your soul. Let him.

Jesus, restore my Union with you. Restore my soul. Saturate me with
your Love; saturate me with your Life.

Linger there for a moment.

> I stand at the door. I knock. If you hear me
> call and open the door, I'll come right in.
> —REVELATION 3:20 THE MESSAGE

AM

Begin with settling down. Take a long breath.

As I enter a new day, what do I need to let go of—what is weighing on my heart?

_____

_____

_____

_____

Pause, and give it to God. Let it go.

What do I need from God today?

_____

_____

_____

_____

Pause, and ask for it.

God promises to fill and strengthen you. Receive it.

Jesus, restore my Union with you. I receive your Love. I receive your Life. Strengthen me.

Linger there for a moment.

Where is Jesus "knocking" in your life?

PM

Begin with settling down. Take a long breath.

To enter this afternoon or evening with peace, what do I need to let go of? (Do any worries, fears, or regrets come to mind?)

_____

_____

_____

_____

Pause, and give it to God. Let it go.

At this point in my afternoon or evening, what do I need from God?

_____

_____

_____

_____

Pause, and ask.

God promises to restore your soul. Let him.

Jesus, restore my Union with you. Restore my soul. Saturate me with your Love; saturate me with your Life.

Linger there for a moment.

Trust the LORD! He is your helper and your shield.
—PSALM 115:9 NLT

AM

Begin with settling down. Take a long breath.

As I enter a new day, what do I need to let go of—what is weighing on my heart?

_____

_____

_____

_____

Pause, and give it to God. Let it go.

What do I need from God today?

_____

_____

_____

_____

Pause, and ask for it.

God promises to fill and strengthen you. Receive it.

Jesus, restore my Union with you. I receive your Love. I receive your Life. Strengthen me.

Linger there for a moment.

God has not abandoned you. You have
not blown it. Cry out to him.

PM

Begin with settling down. Take a long breath.

To enter this afternoon or evening with peace, what do I need to let go
of? (Do any worries, fears, or regrets come to mind?)

_____

_____

_____

_____

Pause, and give it to God. Let it go.

At this point in my afternoon or evening, what do I need from God?

_____

_____

_____

_____

Pause, and ask.

God promises to restore your soul. Let him.

Jesus, restore my Union with you. Restore my soul. Saturate me with
your Love; saturate me with your Life.

Linger there for a moment.

Today when you hear his voice,
don't harden your hearts.

—HEBREWS 3:15 NLT

AM

Begin with settling down. Take a long breath.

As I enter a new day, what do I need to let go of—what is weighing on
my heart?

_____

_____

_____

_____

Pause, and give it to God. Let it go.

What do I need from God today?

_____

_____

_____

_____

Pause, and ask for it.

God promises to fill and strengthen you. Receive it.

Jesus, restore my Union with you. I receive your Love. I receive your
Life. Strengthen me.

Linger there for a moment.

Prayer is entering into conversational
intimacy with God.

PM

Begin with settling down. Take a long breath.

To enter this afternoon or evening with peace, what do I need to let go
of? (Do any worries, fears, or regrets come to mind?)

_____

_____

_____

_____

Pause, and give it to God. Let it go.

At this point in my afternoon or evening, what do I need from God?

_____

_____

_____

_____

Pause, and ask.

God promises to restore your soul. Let him.

Jesus, restore my Union with you. Restore my soul. Saturate me with
your Love; saturate me with your Life.

Linger there for a moment.

Worship the LORD in the splendor of his holiness.
—1 CHRONICLES 16:29

AM

Begin with settling down. Take a long breath.

As I enter a new day, what do I need to let go of—what is weighing on my heart?

_____

_____

_____

_____

Pause, and give it to God. Let it go.

What do I need from God today?

_____

_____

_____

_____

Pause, and ask for it.

God promises to fill and strengthen you. Receive it.

Jesus, restore my Union with you. I receive your Love. I receive your Life. Strengthen me.

Linger there for a moment.

Worship is what we give our hearts to.

PM

Begin with settling down. Take a long breath.

To enter this afternoon or evening with peace, what do I need to let go of? (Do any worries, fears, or regrets come to mind?)

_____

_____

_____

_____

Pause, and give it to God. Let it go.

At this point in my afternoon or evening, what do I need from God?

_____

_____

_____

_____

Pause, and ask.

God promises to restore your soul. Let him.

Jesus, restore my Union with you. Restore my soul. Saturate me with your Love; saturate me with your Life.

Linger there for a moment.

He rescued us from the domain of darkness, and
transferred us to the kingdom of His beloved Son.
—COLOSSIANS 1:13 NASB

AM

Begin with settling down. Take a long breath.

As I enter a new day, what do I need to let go of—what is weighing on
my heart?

_____

_____

_____

_____

Pause, and give it to God. Let it go.

What do I need from God today?

_____

_____

_____

_____

Pause, and ask for it.

God promises to fill and strengthen you. Receive it.

Jesus, restore my Union with you. I receive your Love. I receive your
Life. Strengthen me.

Linger there for a moment.

You belong to God; the enemy has no claim over you.

PM

Begin with settling down. Take a long breath.

To enter this afternoon or evening with peace, what do I need to let go of? (Do any worries, fears, or regrets come to mind?)

_____

_____

_____

_____

Pause, and give it to God. Let it go.

At this point in my afternoon or evening, what do I need from God?

_____

_____

_____

_____

Pause, and ask.

God promises to restore your soul. Let him.

Jesus, restore my Union with you. Restore my soul. Saturate me with your Love; saturate me with your Life.

Linger there for a moment.

The LORD longs to be gracious to you.
—ISAIAH 30:18

AM

Begin with settling down. Take a long breath.

As I enter a new day, what do I need to let go of—what is weighing on
my heart?

_____

_____

_____

_____

Pause, and give it to God. Let it go.

What do I need from God today?

_____

_____

_____

_____

Pause, and ask for it.

God promises to fill and strengthen you. Receive it.

Jesus, restore my Union with you. I receive your Love. I receive your
Life. Strengthen me.

Linger there for a moment.

Sometimes we need to remind ourselves that
God's intentions toward us are *good*.

PM

Begin with settling down. Take a long breath.

To enter this afternoon or evening with peace, what do I need to let go
of? (Do any worries, fears, or regrets come to mind?)

_____

_____

_____

_____

Pause, and give it to God. Let it go.

At this point in my afternoon or evening, what do I need from God?

_____

_____

_____

_____

Pause, and ask.

God promises to restore your soul. Let him.

Jesus, restore my Union with you. Restore my soul. Saturate me with
your Love; saturate me with your Life.

Linger there for a moment.

In his great mercy he has given us
new birth into a living hope.
—1 PETER 1:3

AM

Begin with settling down. Take a long breath.

As I enter a new day, what do I need to let go of—what is weighing on my heart?

_____

_____

_____

_____

Pause, and give it to God. Let it go.

What do I need from God today?

_____

_____

_____

_____

Pause, and ask for it.

God promises to fill and strengthen you. Receive it.

Jesus, restore my Union with you. I receive your Love. I receive your Life. Strengthen me.

Linger there for a moment.

Restore my hope today, Lord.

PM

Begin with settling down. Take a long breath.

To enter this afternoon or evening with peace, what do I need to let go of? (Do any worries, fears, or regrets come to mind?)

_____

_____

_____

_____

Pause, and give it to God. Let it go.

At this point in my afternoon or evening, what do I need from God?

_____

_____

_____

_____

Pause, and ask.

God promises to restore your soul. Let him.

Jesus, restore my Union with you. Restore my soul. Saturate me with your Love; saturate me with your Life.

Linger there for a moment.

I will refresh the weary and satisfy the faint.

—JEREMIAH 31:25

AM

Begin with settling down. Take a long breath.

As I enter a new day, what do I need to let go of—what is weighing on my heart?

_____

_____

_____

_____

Pause, and give it to God. Let it go.

What do I need from God today?

_____

_____

_____

_____

Pause, and ask for it.

God promises to fill and strengthen you. Receive it.

Jesus, restore my Union with you. I receive your Love. I receive your Life. Strengthen me.

Linger there for a moment.

What does your heart need?

PM

Begin with settling down. Take a long breath.

To enter this afternoon or evening with peace, what do I need to let go of? (Do any worries, fears, or regrets come to mind?)

_____

_____

_____

_____

Pause, and give it to God. Let it go.

At this point in my afternoon or evening, what do I need from God?

_____

_____

_____

_____

Pause, and ask.

God promises to restore your soul. Let him.

Jesus, restore my Union with you. Restore my soul. Saturate me with your Love; saturate me with your Life.

Linger there for a moment.

Call on me in the day of trouble; I will deliver you.
—PSALM 50:15

AM

Begin with settling down. Take a long breath.

As I enter a new day, what do I need to let go of—what is weighing on
my heart?

_____

_____

_____

_____

Pause, and give it to God. Let it go.

What do I need from God today?

_____

_____

_____

_____

Pause, and ask for it.

God promises to fill and strengthen you. Receive it.

Jesus, restore my Union with you. I receive your Love. I receive your
Life. Strengthen me.

Linger there for a moment.

Your trials are actually opportunities to watch God move.

PM

Begin with settling down. Take a long breath.

To enter this afternoon or evening with peace, what do I need to let go of? (Do any worries, fears, or regrets come to mind?)

_____

_____

_____

_____

Pause, and give it to God. Let it go.

At this point in my afternoon or evening, what do I need from God?

_____

_____

_____

_____

Pause, and ask.

God promises to restore your soul. Let him.

Jesus, restore my Union with you. Restore my soul. Saturate me with your Love; saturate me with your Life.

Linger there for a moment.

In you, LORD my God, I put my trust.
—PSALM 25:1

AM

Begin with settling down. Take a long breath.

As I enter a new day, what do I need to let go of—what is weighing on my heart?

_____

_____

_____

_____

Pause, and give it to God. Let it go.

What do I need from God today?

_____

_____

_____

_____

Pause, and ask for it.

God promises to fill and strengthen you. Receive it.

Jesus, restore my Union with you. I receive your Love. I receive your Life. Strengthen me.

Linger there for a moment.

What is holding your attention right now?

PM

Begin with settling down. Take a long breath.

To enter this afternoon or evening with peace, what do I need to let go of? (Do any worries, fears, or regrets come to mind?)

_____

_____

_____

_____

Pause, and give it to God. Let it go.

At this point in my afternoon or evening, what do I need from God?

_____

_____

_____

_____

Pause, and ask.

God promises to restore your soul. Let him.

Jesus, restore my Union with you. Restore my soul. Saturate me with your Love; saturate me with your Life.

Linger there for a moment.

Lord, to whom shall we go? You have
the words of eternal life.
—JOHN 6:68

AM

Begin with settling down. Take a long breath.

As I enter a new day, what do I need to let go of—what is weighing on
my heart?

_____

_____

_____

_____

Pause, and give it to God. Let it go.

What do I need from God today?

_____

_____

_____

_____

Pause, and ask for it.

God promises to fill and strengthen you. Receive it.

Jesus, restore my Union with you. I receive your Love. I receive your
Life. Strengthen me.

Linger there for a moment.

Are you listening more to the news
than you are listening to Jesus?

PM

Begin with settling down. Take a long breath.

To enter this afternoon or evening with peace, what do I need to let go
of? (Do any worries, fears, or regrets come to mind?)

_____

_____

_____

_____

Pause, and give it to God. Let it go.

At this point in my afternoon or evening, what do I need from God?

_____

_____

_____

_____

Pause, and ask.

God promises to restore your soul. Let him.

Jesus, restore my Union with you. Restore my soul. Saturate me with
your Love; saturate me with your Life.

Linger there for a moment.

The eyes of the LORD are on those who fear him,
on those whose hope is in his unfailing love.
—PSALM 33:18

AM

Begin with settling down. Take a long breath.

As I enter a new day, what do I need to let go of—what is weighing on my heart?

_____

_____

_____

_____

Pause, and give it to God. Let it go.

What do I need from God today?

_____

_____

_____

_____

Pause, and ask for it.

God promises to fill and strengthen you. Receive it.

Jesus, restore my Union with you. I receive your Love. I receive your Life. Strengthen me.

Linger there for a moment.

God's love will never, ever fail you.

PM

Begin with settling down. Take a long breath.

To enter this afternoon or evening with peace, what do I need to let go of? (Do any worries, fears, or regrets come to mind?)

_____

_____

_____

_____

Pause, and give it to God. Let it go.

At this point in my afternoon or evening, what do I need from God?

_____

_____

_____

_____

Pause, and ask.

God promises to restore your soul. Let him.

Jesus, restore my Union with you. Restore my soul. Saturate me with your Love; saturate me with your Life.

Linger there for a moment.

Everything is possible with God.
—MARK 10:27 NLT

AM

Begin with settling down. Take a long breath.

As I enter a new day, what do I need to let go of—what is weighing on my heart?

_____

_____

_____

_____

Pause, and give it to God. Let it go.

What do I need from God today?

_____

_____

_____

_____

Pause, and ask for it.

God promises to fill and strengthen you. Receive it.

Jesus, restore my Union with you. I receive your Love. I receive your Life. Strengthen me.

Linger there for a moment.

You aren't meant to figure life out on
your own. You have God.

PM

Begin with settling down. Take a long breath.

To enter this afternoon or evening with peace, what do I need to let go
of? (Do any worries, fears, or regrets come to mind?)

_____

_____

_____

_____

Pause, and give it to God. Let it go.

At this point in my afternoon or evening, what do I need from God?

_____

_____

_____

_____

Pause, and ask.

God promises to restore your soul. Let him.

Jesus, restore my Union with you. Restore my soul. Saturate me with
your Love; saturate me with your Life.

Linger there for a moment.

For the LORD takes delight in his people;
he crowns the humble with victory.
—PSALM 149:4

AM

Begin with settling down. Take a long breath.

As I enter a new day, what do I need to let go of—what is weighing on my heart?

_____

_____

_____

_____

Pause, and give it to God. Let it go.

What do I need from God today?

_____

_____

_____

_____

Pause, and ask for it.

God promises to fill and strengthen you. Receive it.

Jesus, restore my Union with you. I receive your Love. I receive your Life. Strengthen me.

Linger there for a moment.

Pausing is an act of humility.

PM

Begin with settling down. Take a long breath.

To enter this afternoon or evening with peace, what do I need to let go of? (Do any worries, fears, or regrets come to mind?)

_____

_____

_____

_____

Pause, and give it to God. Let it go.

At this point in my afternoon or evening, what do I need from God?

_____

_____

_____

_____

Pause, and ask.

God promises to restore your soul. Let him.

Jesus, restore my Union with you. Restore my soul. Saturate me with your Love; saturate me with your Life.

Linger there for a moment.

Above everything else guard your heart,
because from it flow the springs of life.
—Proverbs 4:23 isv

AM

Begin with settling down. Take a long breath.

As I enter a new day, what do I need to let go of—what is weighing on my heart?

Pause, and give it to God. Let it go.

What do I need from God today?

Pause, and ask for it.

God promises to fill and strengthen you. Receive it.

Jesus, restore my Union with you. I receive your Love. I receive your Life. Strengthen me.

Linger there for a moment.

Pausing is one way we guard our
hearts from the crazy world.

PM

Begin with settling down. Take a long breath.

To enter this afternoon or evening with peace, what do I need to let go
of? (Do any worries, fears, or regrets come to mind?)

_____

_____

_____

_____

Pause, and give it to God. Let it go.

At this point in my afternoon or evening, what do I need from God?

_____

_____

_____

_____

Pause, and ask.

God promises to restore your soul. Let him.

Jesus, restore my Union with you. Restore my soul. Saturate me with
your Love; saturate me with your Life.

Linger there for a moment.

Let us run with perseverance the race marked
out for us, fixing our eyes on Jesus.
—HEBREWS 12:1–2

AM

Begin with settling down. Take a long breath.

As I enter a new day, what do I need to let go of—what is weighing on
my heart?

_____

_____

_____

_____

Pause, and give it to God. Let it go.

What do I need from God today?

_____

_____

_____

_____

Pause, and ask for it.

God promises to fill and strengthen you. Receive it.

Jesus, restore my Union with you. I receive your Love. I receive your
Life. Strengthen me.

Linger there for a moment.

Pause and set your heart's gaze back on Jesus.

PM

Begin with settling down. Take a long breath.

To enter this afternoon or evening with peace, what do I need to let go of? (Do any worries, fears, or regrets come to mind?)

_____

_____

_____

_____

Pause, and give it to God. Let it go.

At this point in my afternoon or evening, what do I need from God?

_____

_____

_____

_____

Pause, and ask.

God promises to restore your soul. Let him.

Jesus, restore my Union with you. Restore my soul. Saturate me with your Love; saturate me with your Life.

Linger there for a moment.

Keep putting into practice all you learned and received
from me. . . . Then the God of peace will be with you.

—PHILIPPIANS 4:9 NLT

AM

Begin with settling down. Take a long breath.

As I enter a new day, what do I need to let go of—what is weighing on
my heart?

_____

_____

_____

_____

Pause, and give it to God. Let it go.

What do I need from God today?

_____

_____

_____

_____

Pause, and ask for it.

God promises to fill and strengthen you. Receive it.

Jesus, restore my Union with you. I receive your Love. I receive your
Life. Strengthen me.

Linger there for a moment.

You've made it ninety days! Well done! Now keep going!

PM

Begin with settling down. Take a long breath.

To enter this afternoon or evening with peace, what do I need to let go of? (Do any worries, fears, or regrets come to mind?)

_____

_____

_____

_____

Pause, and give it to God. Let it go.

At this point in my afternoon or evening, what do I need from God?

_____

_____

_____

_____

Pause, and ask.

God promises to restore your soul. Let him.

Jesus, restore my Union with you. Restore my soul. Saturate me with your Love; saturate me with your Life.

Linger there for a moment.

About the Author

J ohn Eldredge is a bestselling author, a counselor, and a teacher. He is
also president of Wild at Heart, a ministry devoted to helping people
discover the heart of God, recover their own hearts in God's love, and
learn to live in God's kingdom. John and his wife, Stasi, live in Colorado
Springs, Colorado.